"If you believe that pe _ ...u history worth mentioning, it's easy to believe they have no humanity worth defending."

—William Loren Katz

Abandoned History Series

This book is part of the Abandoned History Series published by the Museum of disABILITY History, People Inc., and People Ink Press.

Due to a general reluctance to discuss the way those in need were treated in the past, records and memories of the institutions that served the poor, sick, and disabled are fading into the past—into the world of abandoned history.

The Museum of disABILITY History is committed to preserving the important historical record of these almost-forgotten institutions.

This book is a part of that effort.

Designer: Rachel Bridges
Editor: James M. Boles

Publisher: Museum of disABILITY History

ISBN: 978-0-9862182-8-6
Library of Congress Control Number: 2016950239

People Ink Press
in association with the
Museum of disABILITY History
3826 Main Street
Buffalo, New York 14226

PEOPLE INK PRESS

Beautiful Children
The Story of the Elm Hill School and Home for Feebleminded Children and Youth

Diana M. Katovitch

Editor's note: Historical research about disability involves the use of antiquated terms and discussion of outdated attitudes. These are retained throughout the book for the sake of historical accuracy; no offense is intended towards any individual or group.

"(The children) came to the institution, as almost all idiots are, as helpless in their personal decencies as the veriest infant, and far more disgusting to the eye and every sense of the beholder; but they have been taught to dress decently, to maintain personal cleanliness, and to observe the proprieties of life to such a degree, that the teacher and proprietor of the establishment, who had witnessed all the transformation, could not but look on them and speak of them now, as 'beautiful children.'"

Institution for Imbeciles and Idiots, Barre, Massachusetts, 1850

Dedication

My grandmother had two sisters who were diagnosed with significant developmental disabilities. Mary lived her entire life at home and Rosemary lived with my great-grandmother until she was placed in a nursing home due to poor health at the end of her life.

In loving memory of my great-aunts, nearly lost to memory in the bustle of life, Mary J. Davlin (1914–1918) and Rosemary Davlin (1924–1970).

Table of Contents

On Reading History: Information for the Reader

First, let me define some of the terms used in the book.

- *Feebleminded*: An umbrella term to describe people with intellectual disability
- *Idiot:* A person diagnosed with a significant intellectual disability
- *Imbecile*: A person diagnosed with a moderate intellectual disability
- *Moron:* A term coined in the early 1900s to describe a person with a mild intellectual disability
- *Mongoloid:* An individual diagnosed with Down Syndrome

When I began to research this book, I realized that I would need to set aside my modern sensibilities if I was going write the history of Elm Hill the way that it happened. Part of this challenge was deciding what to do about antiquated language about disability. The terms *feebleminded, idiot, imbecile* and *moron* are now insulting and pejorative, used to describe outrageous stupidity. Until the 1950s, however, they were actually accepted medical terms to describe intellectual disabilities. They were replaced around the middle of the twentieth century by what was considered a kinder term - *mental retardation.* The terms *mental retardation* or *retarded* are now considered offensive, and the preferred terms are now intellectual and developmental disabilities. Obviously in the quotes, the old terms will be used. I have also used the terms at times in the narrative for historical accuracy. Dr. Hervey Wilbur, the founder of Elm Hill, and his successor, Dr. George Brown used these terms and the information available to them to describe their students and their disabilities. Some of their observations seem cold and harsh. But the doctors and their contemporaries regarded their students' disabilities as illnesses, illnesses they needed to treat. They described a student with a developmental disability in the same detached way that they would describe symptoms if he had pneumonia. Again, these descriptions are used for historical accuracy and are not intended to offend.

Why does a term become offensive in the first place? A term is offensive when it describes a demeaning, devalued state, a state that no one wants to be in. So, is the word offensive or what the word implies? I think most people would agree that it is the negative meaning that causes pain, not the word itself.

Now, in 2016, intellectual and developmental disability has replaced the other terms. What will be next? As disability studies scholar Steven Taylor once wrote: "Anyone who believes that we have finally arrived at the perfect terminology will be proven wrong by history. I am sure that at some future point we will find the phrase intellectual and developmental disabilities to be inadequate and demeaning." [1]

Blogger Rick Hodges summarized the use of language and disability terms in a thorough article on the subject. He quotes Harvard Linguist Stephen Pinker for further clarity. Pinker coined the term "Euphemism Treadmill" for this churning of terms.

> "People invent new 'polite' words to refer to emotionally laden or distasteful things, but the euphemism becomes tainted by association and the new one that must be found acquires its own negative

---

1. http://sath.org/page/Mental_Retardation_Is_No_More151New_Name_Is_Intellectual_and_Developmental_Disabilities/10130/741/

connotations. The euphemism treadmill shows that concepts, not words, are in charge: give a concept a new name, and the name becomes colored by the concept; the concept does not become freshened by the name." [2]

The terms, then, are less of the problem than the attitudes and assumptions that underlie the terms: the assumption that people with disabilities are less than other people. Changing this assumption means that we must confront not just the language but the entire history of how people with intellectual disabilities have been treated and continue to be treated today.

I hope that the reader will appreciate the vision of the pioneers – Edward Seguin, Hervey Wilbur, Samuel Gridley Howe- who challenged the assumptions and believed that it was possible to teach children who had been written off by the rest of society. I hope the reader is able to see the great devotion and creativity of the Brown family, who weathered the many societal changes to continue to provide good care and teaching to the residents. I hope the stories of the residents themselves will help the reader see them as the three-dimensional people that they were – people with families, friends, and interests of their own. I hope this honest, unvarnished history will cause readers look at history with a desire to learn about how it was in the past, so that we can create more respectful and inclusive environments today.

---

2. The Rise and Fall of "Mentally Retarded": How a term that replaced bad words became one – and how to stop it from happening again by Rick Hodges

Introduction

I love museums. Museums are like books where I can walk through the pages. The outside world fades, and stories of the past become vivid and tangible when I see the artifacts, the images, and the documents.

It was in a museum that I found the inspiration for this book; specifically, at the Museum of disABILITY History in Buffalo, New York, the only permanent physical museum in the United States solely dedicated to the history of disabled people. The museum pays special attention to the history of people with intellectual and developmental disabilities.

My first glimpse of Elm Hill was a small, easy to miss reference, just a caption on a small picture hanging on the wall.

The home was tiny, almost Quaker-like in its simplicity. I imagined the "institution" was a small, home-based endeavor, probably of a devout man trying to care for orphaned or abandoned children with intellectual and developmental disabilities out of a sense of Christian charity.

The caption read: Also in 1848, Dr. Hervey B. Wilbur founded the
"Institution for Idiots" in Barre, Massachusetts. The Institution was in a
modest house, where Dr. Wilbur instructed up to twelve pupils (College
of Physicians of Philadelphia).

The reference stayed with me. I grew up in Massachusetts. My
mother became a special education administrator in the late 1970s, in
the days just after education for all disabled children became law in the
United States through Public Law 94-142 in 1975. Massachusetts was
already working under Chapter 766—a state law passed in 1972, which
entitled all disabled school children to education at public expense.
Many of the students in her program came to school directly from the
large, bleak state institutions, and the story of the terrible conditions they
lived in preceded them. At the time I visited the Museum, I had been
a special education teacher for nearly twenty years. I thought I already
knew a lot about how children with disabilities had been educated.

The information on the school in Barre, Massachusetts, was new
to me, and I was intrigued: Who was Hervey Wilbur, and what was the

story of that school? Over the next several years, in between work and other projects, I searched around for information about the history of schools for children with intellectual disability in the United States. There were a few tantalizing references to Elm Hill and the man who had founded it.

Then, quite by accident, I struck gold: an online search revealed that a huge archive of papers from the Elm Hill School was available for study at the Library of the College of Physicians in Philadelphia, Pennsylvania. Visiting scholars could make an appointment to view the collection. This book is largely the result of my visits to the Elm Hill archive and of interpreting the documents left behind by those people who lived and worked there. Later, I discovered online documents and reports, originally written by observers who worked in or visited the school, as well as a valuable cache of information stored at the Barre Historical Society in Barre, Massachusetts. The resources are listed in the back of this book.

Researching in an archive is similar to opening an old treasure chest. Small, seemingly insignificant objects and papers can contain a wealth of insights into the lives and work of people who lived long ago. What I discovered in the Elm Hill records was a carefully planned, well-tended school for a group of children who, before 1848, had never had any sort of formal education at all; at least, no formal education specifically designed to meet their needs. For its time, Elm Hill was a progressive place, proving to doctors, scientists, and scholars that the radical notion that children and teens called "idiots" could learn was true. The techniques practiced at the school could be replicated effectively at schools around the country, including state-funded schools. For the first twenty-five years of its existence, Elm Hill was a symbol of hope for educating children with developmental disabilities.

But even a school kept separate from the mainstream of American society cannot fail to be affected by changing ideas. The early hope and promise of Elm Hill—to educate children and return them to their communities as contributing citizens—was thwarted by changes in public attitudes toward the disabled. Because of their families' financial and social station, the residents of Elm Hill fared better than many other disabled people, but over the ninety-eight years of its operation, Elm Hill changed too.

The archive gives us a glimpse into the whole life of the school, and I invite the reader to walk with me through this story, as if walking through a museum.

People with intellectual and developmental disability have always been part of human society, but because their history has not been widely studied, many people assume that they either did not exist or that they were all locked away. Neither of these assumptions is true. As blogger Rose Woodhouse (2012) writes:

> … Despite the vague awareness of something positive for other kinds of disabilities in the 19th century, I assumed that all of the bad old days were really, really bad…. That people with IDD, especially severe to profound IDD were thrown into institutions and forgotten. Or abused. Or rejected by their families. That no one took the idea of educating people with severe or profound IDD seriously until maybe the 1970's. And, as I read further, some of the old days were bad indeed…. But, by no means were all of those bad days uniformly terrible…. In general, people with IDD lived at home. And often were, to greatly varying degrees, assimilated into their communities (I mean, at least the village idiot had a village!).

Families and communities tried their best, but often there was a longing for more opportunities for the disabled. One of these missing opportunities was a chance to be educated. From its founding, the United States has valued education. In American society, education was, and continues to be, an indicator of social regard. People who are highly valued receive the highest quality education and the greatest opportunities to continue their education. Educational access is greatest for those with the greatest financial resources. Education is powerful; it allows people to move up in social and economic class. Over the course of U.S. history, people who were not valued, such as women, the poor, people of color, and the disabled, have been excluded from educational institutions or consigned to inferior, separate institutions.

Elm Hill extended the opportunity for students with intellectual disability to access the power of education; a separate education, certainly, but one extremely progressive for its time. Elm Hill was never meant to be a permanent home. Even if children didn't become highly educated or skilled workers, the hope was that they would all return home improved (Tyor and Bell 1984).

As American society changed, the mission and reality of schools for students with intellectual disability changed too. The state schools, founded upon the same ideals as the private schools, became places of punishing segregation. The influence of the larger world also reached through the walls of Elm Hill. During the nearly one hundred years of its existence, Elm Hill witnessed the Civil War, World War I, the Great Depression, and World War II, along with the changes these events wrought. Ideas about disability changed as well; in spite of its separation from the mainstream world, Elm Hill's staff and students were affected by these ideas.

The original Elm trees: the source of the school's name (Barre Historical Society).

History, in the end, is about human stories—real people and real events. Because Elm Hill remained small (never more than one hundred residents at a time) and private, the stories of the people connected to it have been preserved better than most. This level of detail is vanishingly rare in the study of developmental disability in the United States. These are fascinating stories of people who had a place at Elm Hill. The teachers, students, and directors have names, faces, and personal histories that tell us a great deal about what disability meant in the lives of real people in a small New England town in the years between 1850 and 1946.

The name of the school will vary throughout the book: although it was officially named The Elm Hill School and Home for Feebleminded Youth, the citizens of Barre, the students, and the staff often referred to the school as "Dr. Brown's School." Although not the founders of the school, a father, son, and grandson—all named Dr. Brown—were the directors for all but the first two years of the school's existence. I will use the names Elm Hill and Dr. Brown's School interchangeably.

Let's step back in time to the small town of Barre, Massachusetts, and learn about the world of Elm Hill.

Chapter 1: Edouard Seguin - The Enlightenment Comes to the "Feebleminded"

P aris, 1793: People shuddered when they thought of Bicetre Hospital, a hospital for the insane. There was talk of chains; were there really people so dangerous that they had to be chained? According to those bold enough to pay a fee and enter the asylum, the men held there screamed, howled, and pulled against their bonds. They believed that the insane were inhuman.

Imagine the horror of the gentlemen doctors in charge of the asylum when challenged by one of their own with an incredible idea: Dr. Phillippe Pinel petitioned to allow a few of the inmates to be let out of their restraints and exercise in the open air. His colleagues and superiors predicted disaster—"Citizen, are you not yourself mad to think of unchaining such animals?"—but, finally, gave permission. The first man chosen had been chained for forty years. When the chains were unlocked, the man struggled to his feet, walked to the door, looked up at the sky, and cried out, "How beautiful!" He returned to his cell that night and slept peacefully (Kirisitis, Platt, and Stearns 2013). A new method of treatment had come to France.

This new approach—known as *moral treatment*—arose during the Enlightenment, or Age of Reason, in late seventeenth century Europe

and later in the new United States. Philosophers and scientists questioned authority and the unthinking obedience to it. People had minds and will of their own and should be allowed to exercise them to improve their lives and the lives of others. Enlightenment ideas were embraced in the United States, even being incorporated into the Declaration of Independence and the Constitution.

Doctors using moral treatment extended the respect of human will and desire for growth to people labeled "insane" or "lunatics." Before unchaining his first patient, as the story goes, Pinel spoke to him as a rational human being: did he agree to being unchained? Could he behave calmly when freed? By using moral treatment, physicians could build relationships with their patients, help them to engage in productive activity, and create plans for rehabilitation and release from the hospital (Kirisitis, Platt, and Stearns 2013).

Edouard Seguin (later Americanized to Edward Seguin), born in 1812, would have grown up steeped in these Enlightenment ideas. Educated at Collège d'Auxerre and the Lycée Saint Louis in Paris, he began working under the private direction of the famous Dr. Jean-Marc-Gaspard Itard (1774–1838). Itard had gained renown by his work with Victor, the famous Wild Boy of Aveyron, and he had been asked to take on the education of another "idiot child." Itard was terminally ill, but he

Edward Seguin (1812–1880) in later life.

agreed to direct and advise another teacher on the methods he had used to help Victor (Stearns 2014). That young teacher was Edward Seguin. Seguin met regularly with Itard until Itard's death in 1838. He then sought the advice of Dr. Jean-Etienne Dominique Esquirol (himself a student of Dr. Phillippe Pinel), who worked at Salpetriere Hospital. Seguin worked tirelessly with his students, in the face of his mentor Esquirol's certainty that "idiots" could not be educated (Stearns 2014).

Instead of approaching the students like an ordinary classroom teacher of the time, sitting the students in rows and teaching them to read and write, Seguin used a method inspired by Itard and expanded through his own observations that he later called the *physiological method*.

Seguin believed that while cognitively disabled children had "sensations, sentiments, and perceptions," their ability to respond to and exercise their faculties was incompletely formed or had been neglected so long that their ability had atrophied (Stearns 2014). So, he began to build, from the ground up, these abilities in his students.

This approach mirrored the development of non-disabled children— learning control of the large and small muscles, experiencing structured sensory input, imitating and producing speech, and developing basic academic skills and general knowledge. Many of these same approaches are used in therapies for children with disabilities today.

The teacher would have the student begin developing muscular control in the arms and legs by performing strengthening exercises. A child who lacked the ability to walk or stand might be placed in a device similar to a baby jumper or held on a springboard to stimulate pushing up and off of the feet. The child might be held up on a ladder by the teacher and use his hands to grab on to a rung to prevent falling. Exercises with dumbbells, clubs, and balancing poles built strength, coordination, and balance. Children stepped over the rungs of a ladder on the floor to learn to lift their feet, walked up inclined planes, used treadmills, or followed footprints painted on the floor to practice coordinated walking. Fine motor control was practiced with small objects—pegs, sticks, and beads—that students were taught to pick up and manipulate. The children were also taught to imitate the movements of an instructor.

Physical activity did not end in the gymnasium; students were taught to bathe and dress themselves (also to help less able students), to feed themselves using utensils, to lay the table for meals, and to do complete vocational tasks, such as garden work, housework, and woodworking.

When the student had progressed enough physically, Seguin began exercises in sensory training to develop a finer sense of touch, sight, hearing, taste, and smell. He immersed the student's hand in liquids of various temperatures and viscosities, and had him manipulate objects of different textures, weights, and sizes. Visual exercises included tracking a small light through a darkened room, maintaining eye contact with a teacher, and identifying colors and sizes of cards and objects.

Stimulating the sense of hearing—distinguishing loud vs. soft sounds and high and low musical tones, intonations of voice and their meanings—gradually led to teaching of speech. Children with weak muscles in their mouths did tongue and chewing exercises. Students with imperfect speech imitated letter sounds and syllables to improve their intelligibility (Stearns 2014, 61–62).

While "normal" people perhaps would avoid exposure to strong smells or tastes, Seguin reasoned, training of taste and smell might begin there with these students, gradually moving to an appreciation of subtle refined tastes and smells (Forbes 1847).

All of these activities were done one on one with a teacher or attendant and in small groups, where less skilled children could imitate more skilled children. The children passed through a schedule of activities every day, working on movement, speech, senses, and academics in rotations. Seguin urged flexibility in the schedule so that the children wouldn't become overtaxed or bored.

The goal of these many exercises was not simply to make the

children compliant when given directions by teachers, attendants, or family members. The goal was for the children to become self-directed; they were to act on their own will. As described by Rose Woodhouse (2012):

> Whenever possible and wherever possible, and however possible, he forced them to make choices and act on their own initiative. This was to exercise the executive function. As soon as they could start to do anything, he had them clean up after themselves, however slapdash the job, and take responsibility for the order of the classrooms. They learned speech by beginning to imitate syllables, touching the mouth of their educator and touching their own mouths. Then they progressed to words and sentences. As soon as they could say something, they had to talk to get what they wanted. Wherever possible, his learning materials were everyday objects.

Seguin's students showed impressive progress. In 1841, he was hired to teach a class of students at the Salpetriere Hospital and a year later took a higher post as the director of the "idiot ward" in Bicetre (Stearns 2014). He continued refining his teaching method, keeping meticulous records, and his work began to capture the interest of scientists and doctors across Europe. The visitors wrote articles about Seguin's groundbreaking work, and Seguin himself published a book in 1846 titled *Traitement Moral, Hygiène, et Education des Idiots* (*The Moral Treatment, Hygiene, and Education of Idiots and Other Backwards Children*). It was this book that formed the basis for the development of the Elm Hill School in Barre, Massachusetts.

In 1866, Seguin wrote *Idiocy and Its Treatment by the Physiological Method* in which he carefully outlined his beliefs about the cause of intellectual disability (he generally blamed stress and poor diet in the mother during pregnancy) and his findings about how to rehabilitate such patients. He built skills systematically, depending on the patient's needs: first building basic mobility skills and strength, then manual dexterity, accurate sensory perception (visual, tactile, olfactory, auditory, and taste) and speech, then teaching reading, writing, numeration, work skills, manners, and socialization.

His instruction was not limited to the children. Staff was instructed to be patient but authoritative. They were taught to watch the children carefully to make sure they were healthy enough to learn and to watch their charges for signs of frustration, which might be lessened by a lighter activity, such as listening to music. Especially interesting were his instructions to hold back assistance and prompting in order to encourage the children to do tasks on their own and to allow them to help other students.

Seguin also gave explicit instructions about the design of the school, from the size of the classrooms and common rooms to the students' bedrooms and dining rooms. He also listed important personal qualities and skills needed by attendants, who would be in close contact with the children:

> The attendant cannot be empowered to punish or coerce children, but to help and incite them only, hence the necessity of choosing for that function women very kind, gay, attractive, endowed with open faces, ringing voices, clear eyes, easy movements, and affectionate propensity towards children. (Seguin 1866)

He was equally explicit about the qualities needed for a matron to monitor the attendants and teachers of such a school.

Superintendents, too, were given explicit instructions about their responsibilities. They needed to ensure that the children were well fed, that their institutions were well equipped for learning, that the proper staff was hired and trained. The superintendent was also charged with publishing reports and meeting with other superintendents on an annual basis.

No one had ever been so methodical about educating the "ineducable" child.

Chapter 2: Beginnings of Elm Hill

"In the year 1847, I saw in a number of 'Chamber's Journal' an account of a visit by one of its correspondents to a school for training idiots in Paris, in charge of Edouard Seguin. It attracted attention, because up to a very recent time the class in question had been regarded as beyond the reach of any efforts for their improvement.... Not long after, as I now remember, I met in one or more numbers of a British medical journal a very glowing account of a professional visit to the same class written by an appreciative hand. It was the work of Dr. Connolly, one of the princes of British philanthropy. These papers were my first inspiration in what has proved to be with me a life occupation."

—Hervey B. Wilbur (George Brown, In Memorium, 1887)

Hervey Backus Wilbur was a man in search of a mission—and he found one in teaching disabled children. He tried a few professions—teacher and civil engineer—before training in medicine at Berkshire Medical Institution in Pittsfield, Massachusetts. He and his wife, Harriet, took up residence in Barre, Massachusetts, and had a baby daughter, but Wilbur still hadn't settled into medical work (Rose 2008). But he obviously continued reading about medical topics, since he read about Seguin's work in Paris, and became interested in trying the same methods in the United States. He sent a request to Europe for any books available on treating idiocy, and in reply received one book: *The Moral Treatment, Hygiene, and Education of Idiots and Other Backward Children* by Edward

Hervey B. Wilbur.

Seguin. Wilbur had found his life's work.

An opportunity for practical work quickly surfaced: a local lawyer asked Wilbur if he would attempt to treat his seven-year-old son, who had been diagnosed as an "idiot." In the tiny house pictured in the Introduction, Wilbur took the boy in with his family and began teaching him according to the physiological method (Rose 2008).

Word spread quickly, and Wilbur soon accepted a second student. The family moved to a larger house on the same property as the original house (the buildings became known as Number One and Number Two) (Annual Reports 1898).

From contemporary reports, Hervey Wilbur was a modest but energetic man who was genuinely devoted to the children in his care. A visitor in 1850 made this observation:

> It was delightful to behold the inexhaustible patience and unwearied kindness with which Dr. and Mrs. Wilbur devoted themselves to the comfort and improvement of these poor creatures, not only teaching and training them by day, but watching over them by night, not as if impelled by necessity or mere duty, still less for filthy lucre's sake, but expressing and manifestly feeling toward them, in no small measure, the tenderness of parental love. And it was painfully interesting to see how the helpless innocents in return clung to their lips, and watched their every movement with all an infant's feeling of affection and dependence. May they meet their reward from an enlightened public and a liberal commonwealth, which their self-denying labors so richly deserve (Institution 1850).

Passion for his work did not mean that Wilbur was not ambitious; he wanted to increase the reach of physiological education. The same year that Elm Hill opened, Samuel Gridley Howe, best known for his work at Perkins School for the Blind, had also been working with a small group of children at the Perkins School. He had experienced modest success with a few children diagnosed with both blindness and cognitive disability and wondered what students without sensory disabilities might be able to accomplish. (Stearns 2014) Howe had been lobbying the Massachusetts legislature for several years to establish a state-funded school to educate students with intellectual disabilities.. Now it was time for New York State to do the same for its disabled population, and Dr. Wilbur wanted to be the first superintendent of that school. The legislation for the funding of the asylum-school passed in July 1851. The trustees appointed by NYS Governor Washington Hunt, John C. Spencer, and William L. Marcy, traveled to Massachusetts that summer to consult with Howe about how they should proceed. Wilbur had shared his desire to be chosen as the first superintendent of the New York State asylum. The trustees Spencer and Marcy spent several days at Elm Hill examining the students, the teaching methods, and the man teaching them. At the end of the visit, Dr. Wilbur was offered the job of superintendent, and he made plans to move with his family to Albany and later to Syracuse. Wilbur lived the rest of his life in New York; he was buried in Oakwood Cemetery in Syracuse, New York. Not far away from Wilbur's grave is a section where state school students are also buried. [1]

Wilbur had a dozen boys already enrolled at Elm Hill and immediately sought out his successor. A young physician, George Brown, and his new wife, Catharine Wood Brown, had moved to Barre, Massachusetts, in 1850. Among the other prominent citizens of Barre to welcome them were Dr. and Mrs. Wilbur.

While George Brown was the one ultimately asked to succeed Dr. Wilbur as superintendent, Catharine Brown was no insignificant figure in the work of the school. Catharine had been educated in Lawrence Academy in Groton, Massachusetts, and wrote extensively about her

---

1. Cemetery records for state school burials date back to 1901. Records before this time are incomplete, and cemetery staff are unable to confirm if students from the asylum were buried at Oakwood before 1901.

work with the students. In this early article, she writes about her first impressions of the school:

> The early friends of Dr. Wilbur were annoyed and chagrined that he should give up his promising position in the medical profession for labors they considered of no value pecuniarily, and positively foolish. During the winter of 1851, however, he was beginning to receive the consideration he had earned, and his small number of anomalous pupils were the lions of the day, visited by all comers to the town.... I was myself very faithless and delayed following the crowd till common courtesy demanded it. But when I came and saw I had to confess myself conquered. I was intensely interested in everything. A boy with fine head and face, large beseeching eyes, clung to my hand, as if seeking my help. Dr. Wilbur assured me he was very low in the scale of ability, but I was unconvinced till I had tried for an hour with all my will power and perseverance to teach him to pick up a pin. Since that fruitless effort I have never lost my interest in the abnormal-born. (C. Brown 1897)

Catharine goes on in the same article to describe the early days of their work in the first two crowded buildings of the school:

> We accepted the charge after due consideration and commenced our duties September 1st, 1851. ... Here then was the workshop where we endeavored to continue the ways and methods of our predecessor, remaining eighteen months before moving to more spacious and better arranged quarters. We were teachers, supervisors, and attendants by turn, with a single domestic in the kitchen. The children sat with us at table that we might seek to cultivate good habits of eating, or in the sitting room that we might direct their ways and continually prune their uncouth habits of body. Our boys were marked types of this defective class, each one an object lesson for our instruction....Such intimate association gave us practical insight of the characteristics, needs, and ways of reaching such darkened minds. When our helpless ones were safe in bed, we sat down to read M. Seguin's Traitement Moral, Hygiene, et Education Des Idiots (C. Brown, 1897)

The Brown family maintained ownership and supervision of Elm Hill for the next ninety-five years. The insights gathered there influenced the education and treatment of people with intellectual disabilities across the United States.

Chapter 3: The Students and Doctor Brown

T he school began to grow under Dr. and Mrs. Brown's administration. The first students were boys, but the school soon became coeducational. Mrs. Brown described the first female pupil this way:

...Here (in the building called Number Two) was received the first girl pupil described in the Record as most unprepossessing in appearance, but well developed in form and head well proportioned. Eyes dull, face wearing an unmeaning grin, skin tanned by exposure to the sun, lips and chin sore from constant drooling. Articulation imperfect and words scanty, barely enough to express simple wants, all movements awkward and gait halting. Exceedingly willful and disobedient, never hesitating to use force to obtain her desires when refused. Fond of running away, and cunning in eluding vigilance of caretakers. Had been subject to frequent epileptic attacks from birth. (Annual Reports 1898).

The staff of Elm Hill had the fortunate experience of knowing students and their families over an extended time. In the same report, Mrs. Brown wrote that this girl's nephew was also admitted to Elm Hill with a diagnosis of epilepsy forty years later.

Dr. George Brown and Mrs. Catharine Brown (images courtesy of the Barre Historical Society, Barre, Massachusetts).

As each student was received into the school, their name and important medical history was recorded in a student register. Later, Dr. Brown often recorded longer observations and reflections about each case in a series of notebooks.[2] Dr. Brown noted each incoming student's current abilities, family history (with special note of other disabled relatives), and improvement over time.

There were seven columns in the register: Name, Received (date of admission), Age, Sex, Type (disability label), Cause, and Abnormal Heredity. The first four columns were filled out for each student, and they were usually given a label. The most common labels were "feeble-minded," "epilepsy," "idiocy," "imbecility," and "insanity." Brown did not list a cause for disability for every resident; for example, students with Down Syndrome were listed in the register as "mongoloid" and any other explanation seemed to be unnecessary to determine the cause of the student's disability. Some causes are still recognizable as causing brain damage if untreated, such as hydrocephalus, congenital

2. I suspect that Catharine Brown might have transcribed the doctor's notes; the handwriting in the notebooks is similar to the handwriting in a diary kept by Catharine Brown, currently owned by Lucy Allen of Barre, Massachusetts.

hypothyroidism (listed as cretinism), or epilepsy. Other causes are surprising and reflect the limited medical information of the time. If a mother was in a weakened state, ate a poor diet, or had a severe shock during pregnancy, Dr. Brown often listed it as a cause of her child's disability. Excessive masturbation (in one case listed as "solitary vice") was also blamed for causing disability, especially in boys.

A few students on every page had notations under abnormal heredity. Brown noted whether the resident had relatives who were insane, alcoholic, or excessively nervous. Even residents with impeccable bloodlines didn't escape scrutiny. A resident named Henry Earle had this note under abnormal heredity:

Dr. Earle (the resident's father) in rigorous health but on…mother's side were indications of hyper-delicacy of physical organization often observed in old families of "blue blood."

The notebooks are a valuable source of information about the students. The notes for a resident named Estelle Chancellor are typical of Dr. Brown's style.

Estelle Chancellor

June 25/70 Rec'd a girl of 13 years. Idle as girls of her age usually, head normal in shape, … regular, skin dark and rough, eyesight defective, at times crossed and vision variable in power. Some days apparently good as any one's and other times hardly able to perceive the words in a book. If the subject under discussion, or a lack of interest in the lesson, the defect is much greater. It appeared wholly dependent on the nervous will power. She knew a few printed words and could spell more. Her language and articulation were tolerably good, gait nervous and awkward, could partially dress herself and had no ability for useful employment or helpfulness. Pleasant in disposition with a tolerable comprehension of truthfulness. She often told …so totally false, give such a plausible coloring to the matter in cases where there was no motive for the fabrication. What some perversity of moral organization was so clearly indicated. Her mother said she could give no definite cause for her mental condition, unless her own general nervous excitation and feeble health during pregnancy. Was married in her teens and, as is so frequently the case, has almost total ignorance of the physiological laws of her being.

These she deeply lamented. E was her oldest child born during the first year of her married life. Three other daughters were bright and healthy.

Estelle Chancellor spent the rest of her life at Dr. Brown's school.

Physiological education was said to result in dramatic improvement in students; this success was the justification that doctors gave to state legislatures to convince them to open state-sponsored schools. Directors of the early state schools knew that the funding for the schools depended on reports of good success. As a result, the state-run schools only tended to accept students with the fewest problems and the best chance for dramatic improvement (Tyor and Bell 1984).

Elm Hill, being private, had more flexibility. They could accept students with more significant disabilities and give them more individualized attention. For example, there was a boy named Charles L. Dutton.

Charles was admitted on May 9, 1860, at the age of ten with the diagnosis of "imbecility and paralysis." Dr. Brown's longer write-up referred to him as a "spoiled child." When he was admitted, Charles's only "method of locomotion" was to crawl along the floor using his knees and hips. Once he was able to walk using the parallel bars, he was forbidden to creep. Although progress was achingly slow, the doctor predicted that one day he would be able to walk "tho' imperfectly." Following the death of his brother, Charles was summoned home, and without the daily walking exercises soon reverted to crawling once again. He stayed at home at his mother's request for the next four years.

He had lost all ability to walk and stand by the time he returned to school. The staff made concession to this, providing him with a wheel chair for mobility inside and a wagon for outdoor movement. His cognitive and fine motor development became the focus of his education; he learned to read and spell well, learned some geography, and, at the time of the report, was learning to write letters and numbers. His dictated letters to friends and family showed "thought and humor in the composition." His fine motor exercises included stringing beads and whittling. Charles's story did not end happily; although in 1871 he was reported to have continued gaining "book knowledge," he developed mental illness resulting in what the records called "mania... as if under the influence of powerful opiates." Charles died on September 19, 1871. It was later revealed that several members of his family had suffered from mental illness, including his father, whose excessive nervousness Dr. Brown attributed to "exorbitant use of tobacco."

Even with the high staff-to-student ratio of Elm Hill, some students required even more specialized care from private attendants. A young woman named Estelle Tayoe Paine, who was admitted in 1889 at the age of twenty-two, arrived in desperate straits, refusing to eat for days ("averring that only animals ate," according to Dr. Brown's notes), but would then gorge on food and water before vomiting.

A series of separate notes recorded her progress during this time.

1888–1889:

Estelle came June 2 – perfectly emaciated and eating nothing, but drinking quantities of cold water which she immediately threw up. Nettie Moran had her for three weeks. June 18, Miss Kendall came and took care of her—for weeks she took food only once a day, then only cold corn starch or a solid custard that she could pick up with her fingers. She made no effort to help herself—had to be dressed and taken up and down whenever she was to eat or ride—In Jan. she was taken to Boston to consult a specialist. In March or April she began to improve. Would try to dress and would eat some solid food—still picking it up with her fingers. She was in good condition all summer and enjoyed outdoor life very much. During the second winter grip was in the family and she was too much housed some weeks and began to fail in health. She showed her peculiarities by doing whatever Miss Kendall did—she would eat whatever Miss K had whether she liked it herself or not, wore clothes as nearly like Miss K's as possible, and would break dishes or tumblers if they were not exactly like those used at the same time by Miss K. August to September —Miss took a vacation (a Miss Abbott had the care of her) and she grew constantly worse so that by the time Miss K returned she was in a very nervous condition.

Several more pages follow, detailing periods of illness in Estelle's life and the extra staff brought in to provide care. Eventually, she settled into a period of health and relative peace of mind: "She improved constantly and was in very good condition. Took an interest in knitting and embroidery, in reading and church going." Later notes found in the Barre Historical Society indicate that Estelle was a noted presence at Dr. Brown's throughout her stay there. An observer commented that she was a "very tall woman who wore a coronet of heavy braids. (She was) a great walker. Strode all around town with her personal companion Miss McCauley." Although she was born in Troy, New York, Estelle was from a famous English family; she was the sister of Commodore Paine, who earned renown as a commander in the Royal Navy in World War 1. She remained in Barre until Elm Hill closed in 1946.

The staff could be extremely innovative and responsive to students who had psychological as well as cognitive disabilities. A "letter of agreement" is stored in the legal and business related files of the archive. The text is below.

Know all men by these presents that an agreement is made between George Brown MD of Barre, Mass and Wm F. Hard Jr. of Concord, Mass as follows, to wit.

Said Hard shall remain at school and duties pertaining to school life with Dr. Brown at his Institution in Barre for one year, commencing August 19, 1885 and said Brown shall in monthly payments, pay him, Hard, one hundred and fifty, said Hard agreeing to make diligent effort to improve in learning and in all that pertains to gentlemanly and Christian conduct.

George Brown, M.D.

William F. Hard, Jr., Barre, Mass, July 23, 1885

A note in finding aid indicated that this was an agreement between Dr. Brown and a worker. This agreement was handwritten on plain notebook paper and looked more like a "gentlemen's agreement" than an actual legal document. I looked further into the story of William F. Hard, Jr.

In fact, he was not an ordinary hired worker; he was a resident at Elm Hill first received in May of 1882. The story of this agreement also reveals the lengths to which Dr. Brown and his staff were willing to go to reach students and help them to improve.

William was described in Dr. Brown's notes as a "very eccentric boy of 14 years, with a well developed body, symmetrical head, and sullen, impossible countenance." He was very particular and had definite ideas about who he was, what he knew, and what he intended to do with his life, much to the consternation of his parents. William was not above tormenting them. Dr. Brown explained:

> (He) had sorely perplexed and harassed his parents who were at their wits end with him and did not know what to do with him. This condition he comprehended and took a malicious pleasure in doing annoying things to tease them, frightening them by suggesting upsetting the boat in which he was rowing, etc.

Brown writes that:
> His father said his education was so far advanced it would never do to suggest entering one of the school rooms....The father, a melancholic man, very intelligent but generally and strangely attached to his boy gave way to all his whims, treating him as an equal to be deferred to evidently afraid to cross him in any thing lest his nervous system become even more unstrung.

How to convince this young man to enter a school for "feebleminded children," then? Dr. Brown and William's father decided that his residency would be described as employment by the school ("W was persuaded to remain with us only because he was hired by his father to do so and also impressed with the idea that he was helping us and paid for so doing."). This arrangement was documented in the agreement letter quoted above. Brown does not misrepresent the relationship; he never calls William an employee. William must only agree to "further himself" if he is to be paid by private arrangement with his father. Dr. Brown also writes that William was extremely interested in games, even playing croquet by himself if no one else was available to participate, and described him as "very patient in teaching when with others." Perhaps William helped other students to learn the common games of the time and so did help support the life of the school. Whatever the reason, it was an arrangement that helped William keep his self-respect while in a supportive environment, and it was particularly forward thinking for the time. Dr. Brown and Catharine Brown did not limit their efforts on behalf of their students to just the campus in Barre. A diary written by Catharine Brown detailed just how far they would go to support their students. Lucy Allen, a local historian from Barre, Massachusetts, was already familiar with Dr. Brown's school when she read a cache of letters from a man named Joseph G. Moore in regard to his daughter Sarah Elizabeth Moore, who was a student there. In August 2014, Lucy discovered and purchased a travel diary kept by Catharine Brown, detailing a dangerous and difficult trip from Massachusetts to Helena, Arkansas, to reunite Sarah (called "Lissie" by those who knew her) with her father in Mississippi. (Lucy Allen wrote an extensive summary of the diary which she shared with the author by email.)

When the Civil War broke out, students from states that joined the Confederacy would have been separated from contact with their families. Visits would have been impossible, and even mail service between the Northern and Southern states was halted on May 31, 1861.[3] By consulting census records, Lucy Allen determined that there were five students, including Lissie Moore, from Confederate states living at Elm Hill in 1860. What prompted the Browns to deliver Lissie to her family in the South?

...The diary that Catharine kept of the thirty-day trip does not address this question until well into the journey.... In conjunction with Dr. George Brown's daybook, however, it is shown that on Monday, March 16, 1863, the Browns "started for Helena Ark with S.E. Moore." Although it was not difficult to determine that there was a student named Sarah Elizabeth Moore who was born in Mississippi, it was much more difficult to learn why the Browns would take her to Helena, Arkansas. Only after considerable research did it become clear that this student, called Lissie, was the niece by marriage of James Lusk Alcorn, who just happened to be a Confederate Brigadier General. His plantation was in western

---

3. Stamps.org/userfiles/file/symposium/presentations/CharlesPaper.pdf

Mississippi, on the Yazoo Pass, not far from Helena, Arkansas, which sat on the opposite bank of the Mississippi River. Helena was at the time under the control of Union troops—but just barely—and James Lusk Alcorn had been imprisoned there for a short time before being paroled. Apparently the Browns left Barre with their student on faith in a letter that was smuggled to them by General Alcorn on behalf of his brother-in-law, Joseph G. Moore, begging them to bring Lissie home to Mississippi by way of Helena, Arkansas. It also seems that the Browns had no idea that James Lusk Alcorn was a Confederate General until they reached Helena. (Personal communication, Lucy Allen, October 2015)

Dr. and Mrs. Brown destroyed the letter from Alcorn during the trip to prevent its discovery by Union troops. Their decision to take Lissie South was not purely altruistic—they had not received payment for her education and care for almost two years—but the lack of a direct travel route, the dangers of war, and the difficulty of traveling with a disabled woman certainly required dedication. Catharine made the best of the difficulties; the diary was part of her efforts. Lucy Allen continues:

Deciding to take this trip would have been a serious consideration for the Browns. They left behind in Barre approximately 24 employees and 32 students; the school with its multiple buildings; and most preciously, their four-year-old son Georgie. On the first day of her journey, Catharine wrote: "I cannot realize that like today will be tomorrow + the day following, + so for three weeks. And who can say what will befall us ere we reach the end of our route, or what shall chance to those we have left behind us."

The trip to the South appears to have been the first time that Catharine traveled outside of New England. She saw it as an adventure and a learning experience for herself and those in her care. She titled her diary, "Tales by the Way of a Trip to Helena in the Time of the War, For the Benefit of all the Folks at Home." Here we see both a desire to educate and to entertain.... Certainly she also envisioned evening entertainments with staff and students where her journal would be read and used as a basis for discussing geography, modes of travel, and cultures. (Personal communication, Lucy Allen, October 2015)

Catharine's diary gives the only written descriptions of Lissie; other than a record in the U.S. Census, indicating she was at Dr. Brown's in 1860 and returned in 1865, two different researchers were not able to find her records in the Elm Hill archive in Philadelphia. Lissie was an interesting character in her own right. She had difficulty walking and dressing, needing help from the doctor and Catharine during the trip, but she apparently enthusiastically shared her thoughts and observations during the trip. On an especially trying day of travel, Catharine lamented, "Lissie's tongue will not stop + I feel perfectly exhausted." While she needed significant help during the trip, Lissie could read, write, and be left alone in the room while Dr. and Mrs. Brown conducted business. When the trio reached Syracuse, the Browns wanted to call on Mrs. Wilbur, the wife of Dr. Hervey Wilbur, who invited them to spend the night with her. Catharine writes: "When Dr. returned to the hotel about 1 o'clock for Miss Lissie, she had rung the bell + ordered her dinner + I could imagine the high satisfaction she took in doing it."

Catharine also noted Lissie's reaction to Niagara Falls. "(N.B. Miss Lissie was full of exclamations the whole day + used up the adjectives so essentially that if Miss B. herself had been there she could have done no better)."

Lissie also remembered her life in the South and shared her delight in seeing familiar landscapes, even if Catharine was underwhelmed with the view. The Browns and Lissie did eventually reach her uncle's residence in Arkansas, although there was initially doubt about whether she could stay because of flooding at his plantation, but the Alcorns decided to keep her with them in their temporary quarters. The Browns received payment for their travel expenses for delivering Lissie, and they welcomed her back to the school a few years later.

There are numerous stories like these from Elm Hill. The Browns treated their students like individuals, and this was the source both of their effectiveness as educators and the lasting affection the students and their families had for them and their work.

Chapter 4: A Day in the Life of a Pupil

Over the years, Dr. Brown's school on the hill grew to accommodate the students and the educational methods used there. The Twenty-Fifth Biennial Report (written in 1898) describes the campus this way:

> It consists of four cottages for children with outbuildings. Of these four cottages, the largest or "Central" building is for boys....It furnishes a comfortable home for some thirty or thirty-five boys and their caretakers, having extensive sitting rooms, dining rooms, lavatories, etc. This block is heated by hot water and hot air. Madam Brown resides in this building.
>
> Immediately adjacent to the main building, and connected to it by a covered passageway from the basement, is the "East Division." This building is primarily for custodial cases, paralytic boys, epileptic girls....A separate yard is provided for this house, and the patients receive every attention needed. The schoolroom for youngest boys is in this block. This building will amply accommodate twenty-five patients.

Across the road from the main building and fronting a large lawn on Broad Street, is the girl's cottage or "North Division." Here twenty girls can live with all possible freedom allowed, having their separate yards for exercise, croquet, swings, tennis, their own schoolroom, etc....A lady matron is in charge of this building with several assistants for her duties.

Very near the girls house, and also but a few steps from the "Central" house is the Department for Epileptic boys and Feeble Minded adults, called "Der Platz"....About fifteen boys can be accommodated here with large sitting and living rooms, and all modern conveniences. A shop room, with tool benches and lathe adjacent, gives the recreation needed by this class, though we think more of walking or riding in the open air and some form of physical exercise for them....Our lady teachers room in this building at present. These four cottages for children form the nucleus of the institution. There are also numerous other buildings; a cottage for the Superintendent and his family, a cottage for servants, in the extension to which is the laundry, a Hospital cottage, fitted in every part for the care of contagious diseases, ready for instant use, permitting diseases to be treated entirely separated from one another (accommodation for twelve cases, with nurses)....We have a large stable, with twenty horses, thirty to forty cows, chickens, pigs, etc. A large assortment of carriages, sleighs, carts. We make great use of the Stable for our children's pleasure. All ride several times weekly, some daily. Some of our children have horses and carriages of their own. (Annual Reports 1898)

The students and staff of Elm Hill followed a regular schedule. Boys and girls were housed and taught in separate buildings, called "cottages" in the literature, although the houses were actually quite large. Bedrooms were private or semi-private, and the Browns carefully avoided the ward style arrangements common in the state-sponsored schools. Each residential building had its own dining room and classrooms. The school also proudly advertised that it had a first-rate system of indoor plumbing in each building; the students' personal hygiene and the cleanliness of the buildings were a priority.

Arial view of Elm Hill, above (College of Physicians of Philadelphia) and a photograph of the Central Building, below (Barre Historical Society).

This photo was labeled the "custodial building," so it is most likely the East Division Building (College of Physicians of Philadelphia).

Example of a private bedroom (Barre Historical Society).

Example of a semi-private room (Barre Historical Society).

A dining room in one of the houses (Barre Historical Society).

Each day would begin with regular rising, washing, and dressing. Attendants worked in each residence to support the health and skill development of the students. Residents ate breakfast at well-set tables with china plates and tablecloths, the intent being to practice eating neatly and to use good manners in a genteel environment. Staff and socially skilled residents would model good table habits and assist those who were still learning. When children arrived at Elm Hill, even from their wealthy families, their manners and personal habits often left much to be desired. Some children had been overindulged and allowed to be slovenly. With others, low muscle tone caused clumsy gaits, drooling, and poor coordination. Since their parents were accustomed to typically developing children learning these skills and habits quickly, it must have been upsetting to see their sons and daughters grow older but still have the unkempt habits of toddlers. It would have been difficult to bring such a child out into society.

The world moved too quickly and impatiently for the children to learn to do things independently. Life at Elm Hill was designed for the children—fundamental muscle movements were taught, tasks were broken down, staff were trained to be patient and positive, and as soon as the children could do things for themselves, they were given the time to do so.

The Browns took great care in staffing their school. Dr. Brown mentions in his 1866 report that many people applied for teaching and attendant jobs, thinking that teaching or caring for disabled children would not require much skill. He countered,

> Then, nothing is truer than that the lower the grade of the pupil, the higher must be the intellect of the teacher; though the very opposite of this has long been considered true, and we have often had candidates present themselves for the office of teacher with the single idea that anybody could teach here….But gather a class presenting all the phases, peculiarities, and strange phenomena that we find exhibited here, and the more philosophical the mind of the teacher, the wider the range of his education, the deeper his interest in the duties of his office will be. I think the universal testimony of those who have thus taught would be that there is something more than ordinarily attractive in their labors.

The daily program was year-round, including Saturdays; Sundays were still a day of rest. Staff and students went off campus for church on Sundays; some members of the Barre Historical Society remembered seeing residents at church services when they themselves were young children.

Daily instruction depended upon the level of each student's ability. The 1900 Annual Report contains the following details:

> We use imitative exercises in the beginning, with sense training. After preliminary imitative exercises, come those to cultivate perception and give knowledge. The defective senses must be stimulated by proper exercises, and brought as nearly to the normal as possible in each individual case. All this preliminary work, designed to cultivate the attention, the touch, and prehension, leads at length to the learning to read.

A boys' class.

A girls' class (Barre Historical Society).

Once students had gained the necessary skills, their daily activities included structured classroom time. Students in the classes ranged in ability from those doing pre-academic activities ("kindergarten work"), such as sewing cards, using pegboards, and paper weaving, to those students studying in the standard McGuffey's readers used widely in other schools.

> (Reading) is taught by the word method. It has been in use here in Barre since 1848. A certain number of printed and written words are mixed in a box with pictures of the corresponding objects. The child is to place the word denoting the object under its picture, pronounce the word, and write it. He thus learns how to read and write together. (1900 Annual Report)

The Elm Hill archive in Philadelphia has a rare treasure: a journal kept by a teacher named Olive Russell (1889–1891). Miss Russell taught a class of older boys, possibly in the Der Platz building.

She records the different assignments and techniques she used with her students. The following are notes from a typical day:

Saturday April 6th, AM, 1889
Devotional exercises
Read from Nat. Hist. book account of three different kinds of birds,
talking most about scratching birds, as hawks, eagles, etc. Then
had the children tell me that "Birds of Prey have long, sharp claws
and a hooked beak," and after talking with them on the subj. had
them write the above statement (i.e. Washburn, Jaime, Howard and
Hakon) Started Clarence on his writing L's and M's. Started Edward
Pierce on beadwork, sorting them first into cubes, cyl., and beads.
Then came to the writers and heard them read what they had written
and gave a reading lesson from readers to be read through once, and
spelling words studied. Then helped Howard somewhat with his
letter. Came to Clarence and helped him in writing gave Edgar a
start in writing (before that on beadwork) and set Edward Pierce to
making 6's, 4's, and a's.

She reflected upon her classroom practice and made plans for the
future. She described her plans in the excerpt below:

General "92" program

Tuesday: Letter day for Clarence and Edgar
Thursday: Letter day for Sanders
Friday: Letter day for Howard
Saturday: Clay modeling

Each day in "92" I plan to first give each child (except the one I
wish to devote myself especially) busy work—work they can do
alone. Then, I give one child individual attention for his share of
the morning's time. After that time is up he is given busy work and
another child comes under my instruction—so on, until all have had
their share of individual attention. Recess takes place from 10 AM to
10.15, when Clarence, Sanders, and Stanley go out for that time.
At 11:30 I have my "Little Drill" —consisting of Elliot, Rob, Tom,
(unknown) and Stanley. This lasts until 12

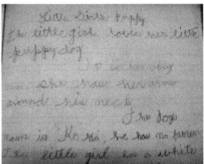

An example of a writing exercise: the teacher gave the student the picture and the student wrote a paragraph describing and elaborating on the picture (College of Physicians of Philadelphia).

The students learned arithmetic, apparently by rote memorization and basic calculation. Olive Russell, and presumably other teachers, also had a daily lesson in history, botany or another natural science, and geography in which the students were taught to recite simple facts. Much time was spent on developing handwriting and composition skills, especially in writing weekly letters home.

Olive Russell included longer descriptions of her students in her journal; she writes about their abilities and challenges. One of her students was a young man named Allen Severence. Allen lived at Elm Hill from age sixteen until his death in the 1940s; some of his writing is shared in chapter 5. Olive wrote:

> Allen's handwriting was handsome. He wrote the whole of his letters, but with assistance in the composition. His statements were rarely in perfect English. His knowledge of numbers was very scanty and imperfect. He read in the Second Reader. I do not remember that

he knew much of geography. [There is a break in the journal at this point; further reflections of Allen continue, apparently some time later.] Allen has somewhat improved in his use of English—he now knows a good many combinations in number yet he is very dull in learning numbers. Can only learn by heart and if he happens not to know what 3 and 1 are he is as likely to say 12 as anything else. He reads in the [blank space] Reader fairly well. He knows a good deal about the United States.

Dr. Brown's students had daily physical education and exercise. There was always at least one room devoted to physiological education; eventually, there was a separate fully equipped gymnasium building, complete with equipment such as ladders, overhead ladders, teeter-totters, and a supply of clubs and poles. In the photographs below, the students are performing group drills with poles and dumb bells (Photos from the Barre Historical Society).

Eventually, a bowling alley and a skating rink were added to the gymnasium. Students spent as much time as possible outside; all of the activities were part of their physiological education. Dr. Brown's impressive carriage, restored and preserved at the Barre Historical Society, was used to get the students outside as well.

Photograph of a physiological education room, with a ladder, teeter-board, parallel bars, and a rocking horse (Barre Historical Society).

Physical activity did not end in the gymnasium; students were taught to bathe and dress themselves (also to help less able students), to feed themselves using utensils, to lay the table for meals, and to complete vocational tasks, such as garden work, housework, and woodworking.

Vocational instruction at first took some wealthy parents aback; manual labor was beneath their families' stations in life. By the time of the writing of the 25th Biennial Report of Elm Hill in 1898, however, this objection had largely been overcome:

Dr. Brown's carriage, painstakingly restored by the Barre Historical society (photograph by Lucy Allen).

Now that manual training has gained its rightful position on the scholastic schedule, partly through the writings of Seguin, and largely proving its value in schools for defectives, it is no longer criticized, but the education of the hand before the brain receives the primal consideration as its rightful due.

Educational sloyd, a graded system of handicrafts and woodworking instruction, was used in the school. Projects began simply and became more complex as the students gained skill. The goal was not to teach the children a trade; the goal was to train them to complete tasks, whatever they were, in a systematic way.

Music was considered an essential subject for upper-class children. For this reason, and for the simple joy it brought the children, Dr. Brown apparently played the piano. He wrote this in his 1866 report:

Music we have found a happy adjunct of the schoolroom and the half hour daily given to singing is looked forward to with delight. A good proportion of the pupils sing well, all are fond of listening, and we have seven who take short music lessons on the piano

Photograph of a parlor with a piano. The young woman at the keyboard is not identified; she could have been a staff member or a student. (Barre Historical Society).

regularly, and can play several pieces with credit and satisfaction for themselves. (Annual Reports 1866)

The busy school days ended with evening entertainment, often in groups. The students enjoyed rehearsing and performing short dramas and musical performances. The school had a stereopticon (an early slide projector that could produce "Magic Lantern" shows) with 5,000 different slides. The students loved the slide shows, and this was probably considered an educational activity. Older students might play cards while younger ones sang songs or played games. The students and teachers would then return to their cottages to retire and ready themselves for another day.

Chapter 5: In the Words of the Students

H istory is best told through the words of those who were there. The Doctors Brown wrote volumes about their students; Catharine Brown wrote articles and remembrances; Olive Russell kept her teaching journal.

But in the history of disabilities, accounts written by individuals with intellectual disability are extremely rare, either because people never became literate or their words were not considered important enough to be preserved. There are millions of pages written by professionals *about* individuals with intellectual disability, but there are very few accounts of life in an institutional setting written *by* individuals with intellectual disability. Among the primary documents from Elm Hill, there are many documents composed by students or former students.

Writing was important in the Elm Hill curriculum. It was among the highest goals of physiological education, the result of many hours of preparation and training. Among affluent and educated people of the time, the ability to write well was prized because letters were how people communicated.

Multiple examples of student work fill the archive. There is a folder

A sewing card in the shape of a teacup, labeled "Mamma from Percy" (College of Physicians of Philadelphia).

of examples of "kindergarten work" —small weavings and sewing cards, used to build fine motor control. Even though there are few words on these items, the projects held meaning for the students who completed them. This carefully stitched teacup is touchingly labeled (probably by a teacher) "Mamma, from Percy."

Two letters from former students of Dr. Brown, preserved in the Barre Historical Society archive, are described below. The writers express fond memories and ask after friends, both student and staff, who remained at Elm Hill (Spelling and composition are as in the original document).

Pleasant Valley, Erie Nov. 8, 185_

Dr. Brown

Dear Sir,
I have sat down once more to write you a few lines hoping to find
you well. I am at home once more and am thankful to be here, but
I cannot realize that this is the same place without my Father. I miss
him so much. I have been at home two weeks and wish I could stay
all the time, but as I suppose I cannot. I wish I could go back to you
for Der Platz is the next to home.
I suppose you wonder how I like Warren, well I will tell you my
Dear friend I could not begin to have the comforts there that I had
at your place and I have had to endure a great many disagreeable
things. So much so that I would be willing to work for my board if I
only could get back to Barre. Also what grieved me was the associates
there at Warren. The men all swear and use vile language which
makes me want to get among better people. I am homesick for my
old home at Barre I have always thought of you and Mrs. Brown as
next to my Father & Mother and wish greatly that I was back with
you. Are Mr and Mrs Cook still at the Platz? How is Mr Burdick
and all the rest of my friends?
Will you please give my love to Dr. George and tell him to
remember to stop here when ever he comes west?
If not too much trouble wont you please write to me?
I would like to hear from all my old friends at Barre.

With much love your old pupil, Robert A. Evans.

Dr. Percy Brown also received a neatly typed letter a few years before
Elm Hill closed from a former student named T. Meredith Kernan. He
asks about Dr. Percy's family, describes his new living situation, and
mentions, "…you would not know me for I am getting old and my hair
is getting white now." This man must have been a student many years
before, but he remembers his time at Elm Hill fondly. (Spelling and
grammar are as in the original)

My dear Dr. Brown—
It is very long time an since I left you at Barre, Mass. But now this is the
four places that I had been into an since I left you there. I don't know
what had become of your Father Dr. George A. Brown and his wife and
the family. By now everything has change a lot under your chargevand
I would not known the same place for I know you have more pupils to
come at all the time.

*****

What become of Mr. Hodges the (coachman) and all the horses he
had been taking care of?
I hope you or some-one will write me a nice letter and tell me about
the place that you are now.
Please remember me to everybody.
With my best regards to you and to your family

Your truly friend,
T. Meredith Kernan
June 19th, 1939

The finding aid for the Philadelphia archive listed four journals
among its holdings: one belonging to Olive Russell (discussed in chapter
4), and others belonging to Howard Nichols, Allen Severence, and Edwin
White.

Howard Nichols's journal is a combination of reports of school
events and short compositions about pictures for writing practice. There
are small notations and corrections made by the teacher. Three entries
are below. (Corrections are in parentheses and spelling is as it is in the
original text.)

December 22, 1896
Last Sunday was a very pleasant day. We went to church. The church
was trimmed with greens because next Friday will be Christmas. It
looked very pretty. Dr. van Dyke preached. He wore a long black
robe. A man played violin. The people sang.

Monday, January 11, 1897
Last Saturday morning Miss Throckmorton invited us to go to her room because it (was) Eddies birthday and in the afternoon we went. She lighted her lamp and poured some water into the saucepan. By and by the water boiled and she made some tea in her little brain teapot. She poured it into some cups and we put some lumps (of) sugar into it with the tongs and we put some lemon into it and drank it. We had some crackers and candy. We liked afternoon tea.

January 12, 1897
The Three Kittens
One kitten is on the table. It is drinking some milk out of the pitcher. Two more kittens are chimbing up to the table. They want (some) of the milk. All the kittens are mish(c) hievous.

I suspected that the other two journals might also have been assigned. Upon closer inspection, it became clear that the writers had started and kept the journals for their own purposes. The journalists were Allen Severance and Edwin White, who wrote them when they were adult residents at the school.

Allen Severence was born October 12, 1871, in Hilo, Hawaii. His medical records from the time, and towards the end of his life, describe him this way:

His aunt, Mrs. Parke, said from the first that he was a delicate and nervous child, quivering at every noise. His mother moved to Hilo when she was two months pregnant. Severe earthquakes were frequent and caused anxiety. Allen was her second child and nothing abnormal was noted about the birth. At 10 months of age he had a severe attack of "Brain Fever" after which his head enlarged. He was slow talking and walking. At 2 years of age when getting his late teeth he had a second attack of Brain Fever. He then had backache and attacks of Pettit (sp) mal till puberty. At 14 years of age he rode with his father on horseback 30 miles to the edge of the volcano and returned at 11 PM. The day was hot and he was much fatigued. The next morning he fell in a dead faint and had convulsions. After this he had 7 or 8 attacks in the next 2 years when he came to Barre aged 16 years in 1887.

Following the custom common to educated people, Allen kept track of daily routines, the weather, meteorological information, visitors and events. A transcript of an average week in Allen's life follows. (Spelling and grammar are as written in the original journal.)

Tuesday, May 26, 1903
Ther. 53
Wea. 71
I swept all the halls this morning and dusted the halls, too. I went to school this afternoon and to the drill this afternoon. It is pleasant today. I am going to read to myself this evening. The sun was out to-day. It is cool to-day and to night. Edwin gave me a ribbon for my bible this evening.

Wednesday, May 27, 1903
Ther. 57
Wea. 70
I swept five rooms this morning and dusted the rooms too. I went to school this afternoon. We didn't had any drill this afternoon. It is cloudy to-day. The roads are very dusty now. We are singing for Miss Barnes this evening. I was on duty this evening.

Thursday, May 28, 1903
Ther. 65
Wea. 69
I swept two rooms this morning and dusted the rooms too. We didn't go ride because we had a shower this morning and it is cloudy this afternoon and this evening. I went to school this afternoon and do Geography this afternoon. We didn't have any drill this afternoon. I am going to read to myself this evening. I received my paper this noon before dinner. I am on dusty this evening.

Friday, May 29, 1903
Ther. 58
Wea. 76
I dusted four halls with the floor dusted this morning. I swept one hall this morning and I swept two rooms this morning. I clean the ladies bold this morning. Miss Barnes has gone home for good this morning. I took my music lesson this afternoon. I didn't go to school this afternoon. I had to stay at home to do my work this afternoon. I took my bath this evening. I am going to read to myself this afternoon.

Allen (who was thirty-one at the time he was writing in this journal) participated in regular educational activities, did chores, and had time for leisure activities. As Miss Russell noted in her journal, although his composition wasn't perfect, his handwriting was indeed handsome.

Edwin White's journal was a Christmas gift from friends. The cover was dark red leather, the pages conveniently printed with the dates. In fact, it was identical to the daybooks kept by the doctors. It was a gift appropriate for a young gentleman, a man of station. The fact that he lived in a home for the "feebleminded" did not mean he was not worthy of the same consideration.

Edwin was meticulous in recording his daily activities (capitalization and quotation marks are as in the original).

Tuesday, Jan. 2, 1906: Weather: Pleasant Ther. 19 59-29/27
Wind in the N.W.
Read "The Old" Testament at 6:25
Swept "The Mats" at 8:20-9:30
Split "The Wood" at 10 to 11:15
Studied "The Guitar Lessons" at 12:15 to 2:45 PM
Wrote a letter to Howard at 3:30 PM and sent it over on 3rd at 7:00 AM by Allen
Read "The Papers" and Magazine. A Fair Day
½ moon and Star-light

Thursday April 12, 1906 Weather: Fair, pleasant Ther. 37 57/ __
Wind in "The N.W."
Read "The Bible" at 6:15. Studied "The Guitar Lessons" at 10:30-11.
3 Feelings this AM
Went to bed at 1:30 PM
Read the Christian Herald this PM
Had a Diarhea at 4:30 PM
A Fair Day
Star-light.

Monday July 30, 1906
Wea. Warmer Rain A.M. Fair PM Ther. 71 85/75
Wind in the S.W.
Read "The Bible" at 5:10 and "The Magazine" at 6. Went out
"Riding" at 9:45 to 10:45. Run the lawn mower at 11 to 11:30 and
1 to 2 PM
Studied "The Guitar Lessons" at 2:30 to 5 PM. Went in to play
"Whist" at 6:45 to 8.
Score 10 to 16 with "Mr. Kiser" and "Allen" and "Harry"
A cloudy and rainy night

Wednesday, August 1, 1906
Wea. Fair, Warmer
Ther. 67 103-83/67
Wind in the N.E.
Read "The Bible" at 4:40 and "The Magazine" not.
Rec'd "The Christian Herald" to-day. "Mr. Flynn" came over this
5:45 AM. Swept "The Shop" at 8:30 AM. Walked "around The
Yard" today. Wrote a letter to "Howard" at 7:10. I sent it on the 2nd
at 9 AM "A Fair Day and Night." Studied "The Guitar Lessons"" at
10:30 to 12 and 1:30 to 4 PM

The writings give evidence of a busy and pleasant life at Dr. Brown's
school from its earliest days. While these writings do not show much deep
thinking, it seems that the students felt that their activities had value and
they derived pleasure from their work.

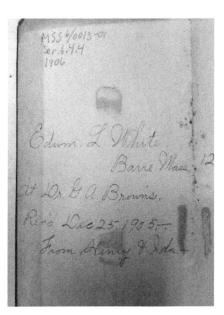

Edwin White's journal and the inscription on the first page (Edwin L. White, Barre, Mass At Dr. GA Brown's Rec'd December 25, 1905 from Henry and Ida).

Elm Hill was not a utopia; obviously, some days must have been better than others. All the written evidence, however, describes a place where the students felt comfortable and at home.

Chapter 6: From Education, to Care, to Segregation: The Rise of the Professionals

E lm Hill was not the only school in the United States advancing the study of educating "feebleminded" children. At the same time that Hervey Wilbur began his work in Barre, there were other doctors who became interested in the work. The first, and probably best known, of these professionals was Samuel Gridley Howe, who also founded the famous Perkins School for the Blind in Cambridge, Massachusetts. In 1848, a few months after Wilbur started with his students, Howe received an appropriation from the state of Massachusetts to open an experimental school for "idiotic children." Howe originally began his work with the students in a wing of the Perkins school. The first students improved so significantly, the experiment was pronounced a success and money was allotted to build a separate school building in 1855. The school was named the Massachusetts School for Idiotic and Feebleminded Youth (later, the Walter E. Fernald State School), and inspired similar state supported schools in the eastern United States. Other enterprising individuals began opening small private schools similar to Elm Hill. Many of the directors knew each other, and they eventually joined in a formal association to explore the topics of intellectual disability and education.

Human progress and innovation were rapid in the 1800s, and the world came together to celebrate and demonstrate human progress in the arts, education, and technology in international showcases called World's Fairs. The first World's Fair held in the United States (called the Centennial Exhibition) was in Philadelphia, Pennsylvania. Experts and researchers came together to discuss their fields of study. Superintendents of schools for the disabled decided to gather too.

> The occasion of the Centennial Exposition at Philadelphia, in 1876, bringing together people of all classes, from all parts of our country, seemed to make it feasible for the first time to call an assemblage of representatives of institutions devoted to the care and education of idiotic and feeble-minded children; accordingly, the management of the Pennsylvania Training School issued an invitation to all other existing institutions in the United States to meet at Media, Pennsylvania, which invitation was favorably responded to. (Proceedings of the Association of Medical Officers of American Institutions for Idiotic and Feeble-Minded Persons Volume 1)

The first meeting was held over three days. Dr. Hervey Wilbur was appointed chairman, and they developed a constitution. What had been a small group of innovative doctors, working independently, had taken its first step into becoming a formal profession. The group called itself the Association of Medical Officers of American Institutions for Idiotic and Feeble-Minded Persons.

Catharine Brown (referred to as "Mrs. Dr. Geo. Brown, of Barre") was formally elected to be an active member of the association in her own right; the association was progressive in that way, including on Dr. Brown's motion, "That all who have been or are trustees or managers of institutions be hereby constituted members. (Volume 1 of the Proceedings) and "ladies of the institution(s)" were also welcome at meetings. At the second meeting in June of 1877—the first at which professional papers were read—Catharine Brown presented her own paper on "Prevention of Mental Disease," and the paper was published in the report of the Proceedings. She would present other papers over the years of her membership.

From the 1850s through the 1870s, these institutions were first and foremost schools. Most of them, following the teachings of Edward Seguin, taught their students using the physiological method. Samuel G. Howe spoke for most of these administrators when he said that these schools "should not be converted into an asylum for incurables," but remain "a boarding school for idiots" (Tyor and Bell 1984). This was the original goal for Elm Hill.

In the 1866 annual report, Dr. Brown writes:

> Of all the large and varied number who have been cared for by us, not one has left without reaping some benefit from his stay here, unless that residence has been too short for even a beginning. Several of that number are now filling stations of usefulness and respectability in life, have served in the army or navy during the war, are managing small farms, or maintaining themselves by some mechanical trade; and from them we frequently receive grateful, warm-hearted letters, testifying their attachment to this one of their homes. Cases have come under our management, where the moral nature was wholly undeveloped, and there was no restraining influence over the corrupt appetites and passions, whose indulgences threatened to destroy both mind and body; and in these instances also a gratifying and total reformation has been accomplished.

The Browns made exceptions in certain cases and accepted adults not for education but for long-term care. For example, in 1866 the school received James B. Milnar, described as "an imbecile 50 years old… sent to us for a home. He was very short, body disproportionate, complexion leathery and cadaverous eyes in shape and color… whole appearance decidedly grotesque." Brown recognized that Milnar had been well brought up:

> His father is a well-known DD and this son has been carefully instructed in the family circle and had developed his manners and intellect to the highest degree he was capable of. He spoke slowly with a persistent drawl, but used good language to express repetition of other's ideas, or childish rants, and absurd fancies.

Milnar was already ill when he arrived at Elm Hill, and he spent much of his time resting or sleeping until his death three years later. Adults continued to arrive at Elm Hill, and some arrived at Elm Hill as children and stayed into adulthood. These residents were called "custodial patients" and came to Barre for care, not education. The Browns described the policy of accepting adult residents this way:

> As a corollary to this arrangement (Note: *accepting permanent residents*), when our older pupils have reached the highest point of mental development probable, in individual cases, we permitted some to give up the daily school drill, for freer home life and occupation, as graduates. (Annual Reports 1898)

By the beginning of the 1900s, however, the policy was revised: now, all residents, including the adults, were required to participate in one session of instruction daily in order to maintain their alertness and skills. In the 1898 Annual Report,Catharine Brown reports "The larger boys have… a Military Drill…which they greatly enjoy" and she references a coeducational "light gymnastic drill" for all students in the gymnasium. The Browns consistently regarded their residents as capable of improving or at least maintaining their skills.

For the first thirty years of this emerging field, the conviction and charisma of the pioneers sustained the original, pure goal of education for the intellectually disabled. But the great minds began to be lost: Samuel Gridley Howe died in 1876, Edward Seguin in 1880, and Hervey Wilbur in 1883.

Another problem within the profession began to emerge. The men who ran the public and private schools were doctors; success for them meant curing people of physical illness (even Edward Seguin called his educational method "treatment"). Their definition of a "cured" individual was one who would be largely indistinguishable from others in their communities. They would be able to work, to run a home, and to manage the demands of everyday life—to function "normally."

Disabilities, however, are not illnesses (although chronic illness can be a disability), and "being cured" is not at all necessary for a successful life. Cure was a medical goal. The students at Dr. Brown's and the students at other schools continued to have intellectual and developmental disabilities and would have varying degrees of independence. Many would continue to need help and support from family members and other people in their communities. The community supports that exist today were nonexistent in the mid to late 1800s. For some people with intellectual developmental disabilities, the only consistent supports to help them be successful were in the private and public schools for the intellectually disabled.

The focus of the Association of Medical Officers of American Institutions for Idiotic and Feeble-Minded Persons began to turn from the causes of disabilities and strategies for teaching to discussions of what to do with their students after they grew up.

In 1886, the opening speaker of the meeting said this:

> The adult portion of this great family of defectives continues to present their interests for adjustment. A large number fail to possess adequate mental or moral conviction to cope successfully with the realities of life and are unfortunate in being without the guardianship of kindred ties to direct them. The possibilities connected with such a life are likely to be freighted with crime and degradation, and more especially is this applicable to the unguarded idiotic female. Happily, the solution of this question is persistently dawning upon the public (Address of Welcome, Syracuse 1886 by Right Reverend Bishop F.D. Huntington).

George Brown acknowledged this reality in his 1886 paper "The Principles of Our Work":

> ...we ought not to hold out to the great public the hope that these persons with radical defects of nerve organization, whose nerve centres are some of them too small and perhaps other centres too large in number of germs or brain cells, thus affecting the whole periphery of the body, that these people as a class are by our training and teachings likely to overcome their defects and become normally developed to these higher themes of the human mind. Yet we do most confidently show the value of the improved condition they may attain under the fostering care of good institutions for them. (G. Brown 1887)

At the same meeting, Catharine asked the following question:

> To-day this social problem, What shall be done with the educated
> imbecile? comes up with greater force… But although the
> feeble body has been invigorated by gymnastic exercises and
> labor teaching, the useless hand trained to dexterity, and the
> intellect quickened to perceive and comprehend simple details,
> we have not yet been able to strengthen the will nor develop the
> moral nature to a degree that can enable the great majority of
> the feebleminded as they pass from our schools to cope single-
> handedly with the evil there is in the world. (C. Brown 1887)

She proposed possible options for this ongoing care: add wings or
cottages to existing institutions, create specialized institutions for adults,
and, for a woman involved in such progressive work a surprising third
option: using existing poorhouses.

> If every town or county possessed the well-organized asylum it
> should have for its ordinary poor, there would be ample room and
> proper care for these still more unfortunate poor, who could there
> bask in the sunshine of greater home freedom than is compatible
> where the abnormal born are reckoned by hundreds or thousands.
> There would be at the same time opportunity among these inmates
> of diverse powers for the interaction of those courtesies and helpful
> sympathies which make life desirable anywhere. The bedridden
> could be waited upon by the strong incapable, who knew only
> enough to do as he was bidden from hour to hour. The trained
> imbecile, the graduate of the school, but still needing supervision,
> could do higher work in nursing and managing those still lower in
> the scale of humanity, —the demented, epileptic, the crippled, the
> uneducable idiot…. Here would be useful the trained ward of the
> state, and all thus occupied would be happy, and by the exercise
> of all their humble powers continually improving, though never
> reaching a high degree of development. (C. Brown 1887)

Catharine was nothing if not practical; by the time she wrote this
discouraging paragraph, she had been working with the intellectually

Dr. George Artemus Brown and Emily Susan Brown, his wife
(Both photographs from the Barre Historical Society).

disabled residents of Elm Hill for twenty-five years. She knew well
that some of her students would never become fully independent. She
could also read the cultural changes as time passed— if families and
communities rejected dependent people as "burdens" other options had to
be found.

  This realization must have been difficult for the Browns. But they
had a school and home to run, and, as previously described, they did their
best to keep their older students engaged in productive activities.

  In 1892, the much beloved Dr. George Brown died. His obituary,
printed in the *Worcester Spy* on May 7, 1892, reads:

> DR. GEORGE BROWN, a resident of Barre for more than
> forty years, and proprietor of the extensive private institution for the
> Feeble Minded Youth, died in New York early yesterday morning.
> He went to New York in impaired health about two months ago,
> and from assurances given by the surgeon from day to day it was
> supposed that he would be restored to health. The community was
> greatly shocked at the receipt of a telegram announcing his death.
> He was 67 years of age. He has always been a very active and public

spirited citizen, respected by all, rich and poor alike, and his death is a great loss to the town…In his professional career, eulogy can hardly overstep itself, and his life work will ever remain a monument to him and to the cause to which it was dedicated. (Annual Reports, 1898)

With the help of her son, Dr. George Artemas Brown, Catharine Brown continued to operate Elm Hill.

Young Doctor Brown and the other men who became superintendents of the institutions were working in a different atmosphere than their predecessors; educating the disabled was now a profession. While the founders of the institutions were inventors and visionaries, the younger men were concerned with running efficient businesses:

The younger men did possess a degree of historical detachment from the earlier pioneering days. They were capable of objectively surveying the profession's past and were astutely critical of some aspects of it. James C. Carson, (Hervey B.) Wilbur's successor at Syracuse, found that "when the training and education of the feebleminded were first attempted the benefits attained were so obvious that certain enthusiasts were led to hope and even to believe and predict that many could be raised to a mental status which would enable them to pass unnoticed in the outside world." Carson and his contemporaries rejected such grandiose aspirations. They believed that only a small percentage of their residents made enough social and educational progress to safely warrant their discharge into the community. (Tyor and Bell 1984)

One of George A. Brown's first duties as the new superintendent of Elm Hill was to represent the school at another world's fair: the 1893 World's Columbian Exhibition in Chicago. The *Barre Gazette* published this account on May 16, 1893:

Dr. Brown's Institution for Feeble Minded
The institution for feeble minded youth brought to its present successful basis by the late Dr. Geo Brown, and carried on by his widow and son, Mrs. C.W. Brown and Dr. Geo A Brown, will be

represented at the worlds fair by specimens of work done by the pupils numbering 75 or more. These specimens of work include letters, composition, two books of progressive arithmetic and writing kindergarten work map drawing sketches, etc . A valuable and most interesting part of the collection sent was the numerous papers, written by the teachers concerning the methods of teaching these children and what is accomplished. There are also specimens of plain sewing and fancy work done by the girls. Photographs made by Notman, of Boston, of all of the buildings were sent. [Author's note: many of the photographs in this book were taken for the 1893 World's Fair.]

George A. joined other institutional superintendents at the World's Fair. Schools for disabled children were a source of fascination for the public; educational exhibits were part of the Liberal Arts Division of the Fair. It was an excellent opportunity for private school proprietors to advertise for new students. This description comes from the 1893 Book of the Fair:

> The groups representing asylums for the deaf, dumb, blind, and feeble-minded form an elaborate display, and one in which are fully illustrated the most humane and intelligent methods of treatment and training. Manual work of a rough description the visitor would probably expect to find among the exhibits of schools for the blind; but to see their printed publications, free-hand drawings, and the finest of crochet work is somewhat of a surprise. A Washington institute for the deaf has contributed a replica of the monument erected at the national capital in honor of Gallaudet the elder, by whom was founded in Philadelphia the first American institute for deaf-mutes. Even from insane asylums are specimens of useful workmanship, for in such are not a few possessed of the rational faculty in a greater degree than many outside their walls. (Bancroft 1893)

The professional change of attitude toward "the feebleminded"— that they were more in need of care and containment than in need of education—became evident at future world's fairs. Consider the change of attitude over the decade between the 1893 exhibition and the 1904 exhibition.

At the 1904 World's Fair in Saint Louis, Illinois, students from schools for the deaf and schools for the blind appeared as "live exhibits"; their teachers actually held classes in the buildings so fairgoers could see educational techniques in action. I was hoping to find evidence that schools for the intellectually disabled had similar exhibits even if Elm Hill itself was not represented, but no intellectually disabled students were present.

> Unlike the exhibits of the blind and the deaf, the exhibit of feeblemindedness at the World's Fair was not a living exhibit. Instead, the Association of Medical Officers of American Institutions for Idiotic and Feebleminded Persons…put together an exhibit representing the work of several public institutions and private schools. (Trent 1998)

The exhibit was placed at a distance from the living classrooms and had ample supplies of literature so that fairgoers could take away contact and enrollment information for themselves, family members, or friends.

Further research into the 1904 World's Fair explained why there were no live exhibits alongside those of other special schools: blind and deaf students were considered improvable; "feebleminded students" were not. The public would gain nothing from watching a class of this kind of "defectives."

Edward Ellis Allen, an authority on the causes of blindness, spoke in front of a group of professionals who worked with disabled people:

> …he reminded his listeners of a position that, at the beginning of the new century, was becoming more prominent: Education could bring most, but not all, defectives up to a level of civilization necessary for participating in day-to-day affairs. (Trent 1998)

The idea that "defectives," even those who had been educated, should stay in segregated institutions rather than return to live and work in the community with their families became commonplace. The professionals and the public believed they would be safer and happier apart from general society. This preference impacts services to this day—too often, people with intellectual developmental disabilities live and work apart from their communities, under the misguided belief that only "special places" can accommodate "special people."

At the same time, an even more dangerous idea began to spread. The future of people with intellectual disabilities was at risk from the very people who were supposed to be dedicated to their rights and safety.

Chapter 7: The Gathering Storm: Eugenics and The "Menace of the Feebleminded"

Under George Brown's guidance, Elm Hill had its golden years. Even though some students were becoming permanent residents, it remained a school committed to helping students reach their greatest potential. But clouds were beginning to appear on the horizon, clouds that still cast a shadow over the lives of people with intellectual disabilities today.

In the early days of the United States, people living with developmental disabilities lived, worked, and were cared for in the community. The local government would provide some support to the poor, including the disabled who could not work: people might receive payments for "outdoor relief" that would help them remain in the community or they could be housed in poorhouses or asylums. While the quality of the care and treatment could be terrible, not everyone with intellectual disability was poorly treated. People with intellectual disabilities, in general, were considered to be harmless; they were just another group of odd and needy people living in the community, and the community was expected to provide some measure of care. In the mid-

1800s, "the feebleminded" were regarded as "worthy recipients of the state's attention," (Osgood 2001) because the improvement of their skills would improve the larger society. The ultimate hope was that students could learn a trade to support themselves, but even short of that goal teachers hoped that, "… an idiot …, becomes, if not restored to society, at least restored to his family, his bad habits are corrected, he is more obedient, more active, in better health, and affectionate to those who have given him their affection and support…" (Forbes 1847).

The residents of Elm Hill had advantages beyond those of other people with disabilities. Their families had the resources to keep them in school for long periods of time, allowing them greater gains in skills and behavior. Even if the children made little progress, family privilege meant that they would have good quality care throughout their lives, either at home or in another private institution. But not everyone with disabilities was so fortunate.

Starting in the 1870s and peaking in the early 1900s, public opinion began to change. People who needed assistance, regardless of the reason, were labeled "burdens" on the community—they consumed time, energy, and money, and gave nothing in return. For the sake of the larger community, the logic ran, "those people" should be committed by court order to a segregated setting where they could be properly—and economically—cared for.

THE COST OF THE FEEBLE-MINDED OUTSIDE OF INSTITUTIONS

Wherever a careful study has been made, feeble-mindedness is found to constitute a serious drain upon the resources of all public and private agencies for relief. Resources which should be used for the relief of normal persons are diverted to the needs of defectives, with the result that conditions which should be made impossible are perpetuated.

All who have studied or have had to do with the feeble-minded are convinced that they inevitably become the dependent, delinquent, or diseased members of their communities, and producing offspring, these are equally ignorant, immoral, and prolific.

In one way or another the burden of their support is thrown upon private or more commonly upon public charity. (The Menace of the Feebleminded in Massachusetts 1913)

Had public opinion simply remained suspicious, maybe the continued progress and success of disabled people would have won the day. But the looming "menace of the feebleminded" and other marginalized groups inspired a time of poor science and cruel social policy.

Disability, addiction, poverty, and criminal behavior, previously attributed to environment, illness, or other causes, began to be blamed on a single factor: heredity. If parents or family members had these undesirable traits, doctors began to predict that the children in these families would inherit them, too. Therefore, people believed, the people who presented a "social problem" (such as disability) would continue to perpetuate the problem if they had children themselves.

Family history has long been of interest to doctors. It is worth noting that when students were admitted to Elm Hill, the Browns noted in the register and medical notes if they had relatives who were alcoholics, afflicted with "nervous disorders," or were living "dissipated lives." Certainly, some illnesses or propensities towards illness or addiction are more common in the first degree relatives of those who have them, but social ills are much more complex in nature than just "bad blood." But to many experts, bad heredity became the single cause for a troubled life.

Therefore, to prevent these social problems, leaders in social science proposed that the so-called "fit" should have as many children as possible and the "unfit" should limit their reproduction. In 1883, the British researcher Sir Francis Galton coined the term *eugenics* (meaning "well-born") to describe this philosophy. People with intellectual disability were counted among the unfit.

Dr. Henry H. Goddard, a psychologist and researcher at the Vineland Training School in New Jersey, was a major contributor to the public fear of those called "feebleminded." He published his book *The Kallikak Family: A Study in the Heredity of Feeble-Mindedness* in 1912. Beginning with a young resident of the training school, given the pseudonym Deborah Kallikak (her name was actually Emma Wolverton),

Goddard claimed to trace her "familial feeblemindedness" back to the Revolutionary War. Allegedly, Deborah's ancestor, a man Goddard named Martin Kallikak, Senior, had a brief affair with a woman Goddard described as a "feeble-minded bar maid." This affair resulted in the birth of a boy the mother named Martin Kallikak, Junior. Martin Sr. then returned home, married a respectable woman, and had other children. The descendants of each line had vastly different outcomes: the children and grandchildren of Martin Kallikak Junior were poor, damaged reprobates (including young Deborah Kallikak) while the children and grandchildren of the other lineage were healthy, well-to-do, and thriving. Generations of Kallikaks were allegedly damaged by the introduction of the feebleminded traits to their bloodline. [4]

Along with encouraging marriage and childbearing of the "fit,"(called positive *eugenics*) proponents also began to push for *negative eugenics*. Negative eugenics sought to prevent unfit people from reproducing by keeping them segregated from the larger community and separated by gender in institutional settings. Negative eugenics also encouraged the sterilization of the unfit; many states actually legalized it. Some disabled residents who wished to leave institutions for a life in the community were required to submit to surgery as a condition of discharge. Tens of thousands of other people labeled "feebleminded," both in institutions and living in the community, were sterilized without their knowledge or consent.

Positive and negative eugenics policies eventually carried to their logical conclusion: *lethal eugenics* or *euthanasia*. In 1915, a doctor named Harry J. Haiselden of Chicago, Illinois allowed a disabled newborn boy, John Bollinger, to die rather than give him an operation that would have saved his life (this is an example of *passive euthanasia*). Notable people—surprisingly, even Helen Keller—expressed public support for the decision. In 1917, a commercial film called *The Black Stork* told the fictionalized story of this decision, urging the public to adopt eugenic

---

4. H.H. Goddard's work has since been discredited. In fact, the story of the "feeble-minded bar maid" was not true. The "good" and the "bad" lines of Kallikaks did not even begin with the same man. For a wonderful investigation into the Kallikaks, see the book *Good Blood, Bad Blood: Science, Nature, and the Myth of the Kallikaks* by J. David Smith and Michael L. Wehmeyer

attitudes; Dr. Haiselden even played himself (as the character Dr. Dickey) in the film. The film was re-released ten years later under the title *Are You Fit to Marry?* In 1939, before the start of World War II, active lethal eugenics spread to Nazi Germany. The first person to be euthanized under the Nazi regime was a five-month-old boy named Gerhard Herbert Kretschmar, who was born blind and missing parts of either his arm or leg. His parents petitioned Adolph Hitler to have him killed.

Even today, the rights of people with intellectual disabilities to sexual relationships and reproduction are discouraged at best, and restricted or forbidden at worst. Those in the disability community rightly fear the return of legalizing euthanasia and assisted suicide.

How did these policies and beliefs influence the residents at Dr. Brown's? The school was coeducational from its earliest days, although males and females were housed and taught separately; this practice was typical in private schools at the time. Students of both genders were allowed to mix at organized evening events. Of course, eugenic segregation by sex and involuntary commitment to an institution disproportionately affected working-class and poor people. Disabled children of wealthy families might be discreetly sent to single-sex institutions or closely monitored in mixed company, but the courts didn't commit them involuntarily.

Involuntary sterilization was never legalized in Massachusetts. Massachusetts did pass laws in the 1940s preventing the "feebleminded" from getting married; even if one or the other of the partners had been voluntarily sterilized [5] I found no evidence to indicate that students at Dr. Brown's underwent involuntary sterilization. Sterilization surgery might have taken place at a family's request during a visit home or during hospitalization for other procedures (sterilization could be passed off as appendectomy or hernia repair), but I found no evidence in the archives that students were subject to such surgery, although it may have happened quietly.

There is also no evidence that the Browns supported passive or active euthanasia. But there is a sad note at the end of a medical record of a little girl named Gertrude White.

5. www.uvm.edu/~lkaelber/eugenics/MA/MA.html

August 29/70 Rec'd a most unfortunate little girl of five years, born with a very imperfect body. She was paralytic, unable to walk or stand, had never spoken, heard imperfectly, and suffered from frequent epileptic attacks. She was very thin though her appetite was tolerably good. Mastication and digestion were imperfectly performed. All of her food was minced and softened and then placed quite back in her mouth. She is tall as average children of her age. The spine is so weak… she is supported by steel corsets.

Her eyes were bright and face wore a very sweet expression.

We cared for little Gertie tenderly as we could, and rejoiced when death released her from her suffering after she had been with us fifteen months. Vitality was strong in the frail tenant and it was at the end a hard struggle to die.

The death of an able-bodied seven year old would have been considered a tragedy; Gertie's death was a blessing and a release. Disability, it seemed, made all the difference.

Chapter 8: Closing the School on the Hill

Following the death of the original, much beloved George Brown, his son Dr. George A. Brown took over as superintendent of Elm Hill. Catharine clearly continued to have an active role in the administration of the school; in the 1900 Annual Report, she is listed with her son as a "Superintendent" of the school. But the years of the school as a place of innovation and expansion were over.

By the fiftieth anniversary of the school in 1898, the number of residents had dropped to thirty (*Barre Gazette*, June 27, 1946). Other private schools had opened, so Elm Hill had much more competition. Public schools began to offer ungraded classes for "backward" children, so that children with mild disabilities could stay at home. Children needing more intensive care could be sent to the public institutions that were cropping up all around the United States, where the cost of care was much lower.

In 1907, Catharine Brown died. While perhaps not as beloved as her husband, she was a difficult woman to overlook, because of her deep involvement in the work of the school and the profession of teaching disabled children. George Brown's epitaph reads, "Noble, generous,

Gravestone of the Browns (photograph by Lucy Allen).

beloved. A Christian Gentleman." Catharine is remembered only as "His Efficient Wife."

Catharine Brown also appears to have been the record-keeper for Elm Hill. In both the Philadelphia and Barre archives, there are few records between 1903 and the school's closure, except for financial records and legal documents. I was hopeful that the daybooks kept by George A. and Percy Brown would contain more stories about the students and staff, but both were used to keep "To Do" lists. Even historically important dates, such as the day of the Pearl Harbor bombing, were not recorded in the daybooks.

George A. Brown continued to operate the school for its small, aging population of residents. In 1911, his son Dr. George Percy Brown, newly graduated from Yale University, became the codirector. Several residents we have met in past chapters were still living at Dr. Brown's as late as the 1940s. Allen Severence, one of the journal writers, was one of them. He died in 1941 at age sixty-nine from stomach cancer and was buried in Augusta, Maine. Estelle Chancellor had the distinction of being the longest resident of the school; she was fourteen when she was admitted in 1870 and eighty-five when she died in 1941, having lived at Dr. Brown's for an astonishing seventy-one years. In the final medical record, the writer notes that she had a younger brother (described as "a mongoloid") who also lived at the school until he succumbed at age forty-five, sixteen years before his older sister. I was not able to find any other records of his time living in Barre, Massachusetts.

Dr. George A Brown died in 1942. He left the Main Building, the Central Building, East Division, and the laundry building, as well as the directorship of Elm Hill to his son, George Percy; by that time, the population of the school had dwindled to seventeen residents, so this was ample space to continue running the school (*Barre Gazette*, June 27, 1946). Another son, Donald M. Brown, inherited the remaining 250 acres of farmland. It would fall to Dr. Percy (as he was called) to close this long-time haven for the residents.

Dr. Percy Brown decided to close the school in 1946, citing the expense of operation, declining enrollment due to the rise of state institutions, and increasing state rules regarding care facilities for the disabled. There were sixteen residents when the school closed.

Clearly, the news that the long-term safe haven was closing was

Daybooks contained in an archival box (College of Physicians of Philadelphia).

devastating to the families of the residents. Family members needed to scramble to find alternative arrangements for their relatives. The final residents had spent many years at Elm Hill, and most were now under guardianship of siblings, who were getting older themselves. A transcript of letters from the sister of Lawrence Abbe shows the typical response of families to the news of the closure:

127 Sumner Ave
Springfield
May 9, 1946

Your letter came today. It is truly a calamity to us all—probably most of all to Lawrence. His life has been so happy and free as circumstances have permitted. We hardly know where to turn but shall go to work right away to locate an institution which we can consider. Can you help us by giving us the names of any such places?
Jennette Abbe

Letter of June 8ᵗʰ, 1946

Dear Dr. Brown,
I have had a conference today with Dr. Tadgell of Belchertown regarding Lawrence's future. In order that he may advise us more intelligently, he would like me to bring Lawrence to see him and we have an appointment for Wednesday, June 19ᵗʰ at the doctor's office at 2 PM…

I do not wish to have Lawrence hear any discussion that would trouble him and so I am asking that you just tell him that I am coming to take him out for a ride—I will explain to him as we are riding as best I can do. Dr. Tadgell has several alternatives to suggest.
Sincerely,
Jennette Abbe

Lawrence Abbe was transferred later that summer to the Belchertown State School. Later letters from his sister indicate that he seemed happy there and was eager to return to the institution after a visit home.

Estelle Tayoe Payne, who had lived with mental illness as well as intellectual disability and needed a special attendant to help her stay calm, was seventy-nine years old at the time of the closure. She was moved to Craig House in Beacon, New York (referred to in the letter as a "mental institution"), which her family felt was a good place. Her family wrote that they wished they could hire a personal attendant for her again, but the high cost of Craig House precluded it. As an interesting historical footnote, Rosemary Kennedy, the oldest sister of President John F. Kennedy, was placed at Craig House after her devastating pre-frontal lobotomy, and her time there overlapped briefly with Estelle's.

The *Barre Gazette* (June 27, 1946) describes the disposition of the Elm Hill property this way:

> Dr. Brown is now tearing down a section of the East building and will offer the remainder of the building as well as the Central building for sale. He is selling the laundry building to Mr. and Mrs. Edward Loughman, who will remodel it into a home.
>
> Donald M. Brown has been carrying on the farm, which he will continue, and he is opening building lots to sell on Union and High Streets. He is to live in the Dr. George A. Brown house and Dr. G. Percy Brown will continue to make his home in the house in which he now resides, but he and Mrs. Brown will spend, as they have for many years, the summer months at their summer home in Rockport.

Image of Ed Loughman's house, the converted laundry building (Barre Historical Society).

Over time, most of the school buildings were repurposed or destroyed. A news article from Saturday May 6, 1950, reports the razing of the Central Building by its new owner, R.T. Curtis.

Dr. Percy spent the rest of his life in Barre and remained active in the community. He was a noted gardener and developed more than seventy hybrid irises during his life. He died in 1971 at the age of eighty-three, and was buried with his parents in their plot in the Barre Cemetery.

OLD AND NEW OWNERS

Dr. G. Percy Brown, left, owner of the well known Elm Hill School for Feeble Minded at Barre who sold the main building to R. T. Curtis, right, who will raze the landmark to make way for two private residences.

A newspaper clipping, showing Dr. Percy (left) and Mr. Curtis (on the right) (Barre Historical Society).

Chapter 9: The Beautiful Children of Elm Hill

Photographs, like literary documents, are not to be taken at face value. Despite their seeming realism, they are actually constructions of the human imagination, made by individuals with particular cultural or economic ambitions. Like a memoir or a letter, a photograph may describe events, but it does so through the lens of the recorder's own experience.[6]

A s they say, a picture is worth a thousand words. When schools for students with intellectual disabilities became custodial institutions, photographs were taken of the patients for their medical files. Others were taken for textbooks to show future doctors what disabled bodies looked like. They were not meant to be artful or displayed. But the photograph albums from Elm Hill were different. Of all the research I did on Elm Hill, nothing was as thrilling as finding pictures of the students. I found only one "medical" style picture (which may have been used for diagnosis of a resident); all the rest were elegant, formal portraits. The residents are carefully dressed and styled. They look refined, even dignified. The pictures were the definitive proof that the residents of Dr. Brown's school were more than their labels; —they were individuals in their own right.

All of the photographs that follow were formal portraits—a photographer was engaged, an appointment made, formal clothing was donned, and the sitter went to a studio. The Elm Hill finding aid estimates that these

6. www.gilderlehrman.org/history-by-era/art-music-and-film/essays/photography-nineteenth-century-america

photographs probably were taken between 1890–1903. A photographer named George Putnum, who operated a studio on the Smith Block of Barre, Massachusetts, took many of these photographs, clearly when the students were living at Dr. Brown's school. If you look closely, several photos have the same backdrop or props in different pictures. Families sent other photos to the school for the photo album; the pictures were labeled with the name of the studio that took the portrait.

These portraits were meant to be *seen*, not hidden away. Perhaps they were displayed in a parlor or parents' bedroom to remind the family of the child who was away from home. The images convey pride, not shame. They are compelling proof that the families valued and loved their "feebleminded" members enough to pay for a good quality photograph, regardless of what the world may have thought of them.

All of the photographs that follow are from the College of Physicians of Philadelphia archive, except for the photograph of Estelle Chancellor, which is from the Barre Historical Society.

Addie Field: A young woman approximately in her late teens, with her hair pulled back and wearing a formal dress with a lace collar. She entered the school in 1857 at age sixteen, with a diagnosis of "imbecility with irresponsible untruthfulness."

This little boy, wearing a suit and striped socks, is named as G. Lowe. He appears to be seven or eight years old.

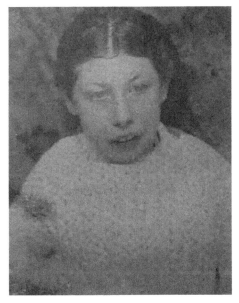

Jeannie Rop: She seems to be around eight years old, wearing a light-colored eyelet dress. Her hair is parted in the middle and pulled back from her face.

This picture was not labeled. This young man, wearing a dark suit and tie, appears to be in his late teens. He is photographed in three-quarters profile.

An unlabeled picture: This boy seems to be about ten years old and is wearing a dark jacket and tie.

This young woman is Katie Bottie. She is wearing a dark colored, heavily trimmed dress, is wearing her dark hair in long curls, and seems to be in her teens.

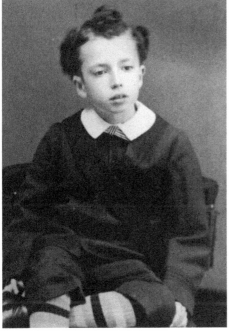

Ralston King: This little boy seems to be between the ages of eight and ten. He is seated and is dressed in a dark suit with short pants and striped socks.

Estelle Chancellor came to Dr. Brown's in 1870 and lived at the school until her death in 1941, longer than any other resident (her story is told in chapter 3 and chapter 8). She was about six years old in this picture, which was taken before she came to Elm Hill. Her short hair is dark and pulled back from her face with clips.

This man, with a mustache and wearing a formal suit, is John Hammond. John was admitted in 1879 at age thirteen. He seems to be in his thirties in this photograph and apparently still lived at Dr. Brown's.

Frank Coolidge: Pictured wearing a long coat and a tie, Frank was identified as a "working student, helped for many years in the garden."

This man is William R. Whiting. He is wearing a dark suit and has a well-trimmed mustache and beard. A note under the picture read, "Hydrocephalus, was here from childhood to old age."

This little girl, wearing a striped dress with dark rosettes down the front, is listed as Susie Clark. A note under the picture reads, "Dancing, harmonicas, slightly mad." She is the only child who is smiling in her picture.

This young boy of about ten years old is wearing a long dark coat and holding a dark hat. He is listed as William Sanborne.

A photograph of two young boys both wearing dark suits; one of the boys is seated on a hassock, and the other is standing. They both appear to be in late childhood. It is unknown whether the boys were related or if they were both residents of Dr. Brown's school. The names written under the pictures were illegible.

This young woman is listed as Margaret Welch. She is wearing a high ruffled collar and her long dark hair is pulled back from her face. She entered Elm Hill in 1906 Under the picture, someone wrote, "Never spoke. Played with dolls." The Frontenac Historical Society in Union Springs, New York (my home town), found that she was born in Richfield Springs, New York, and had a family connection to Union Springs.

This may be Lawrence Abbe as a child (his story is told in chapter 8), but the picture is labeled "Lawrence or Ned." He is wearing a dark hat and a dark coat, with a bow tied under his chin.

This young boy is Angus Cameron Plume. Touchingly, these photos were sent to Dr. Brown's school after his death in late childhood. Angus is leaning on one arm, wearing a dark suit, with a large white collar and coat.

This little boy has haunted me from the first time I saw his picture, because he looks so vulnerable and wistful. The picture is labeled Hoffin Worcester. He is small, so his age is uncertain, and is propped on a pillow, as though he is not able to hold up his head independently. Clearly, the staff at Elm Hill took great care with him.

Chapter 10: Barre Today

The town of Barre, Massachusetts, is in the center of the state, and it still has a sleepy, rural feel. There is little remaining evidence of Dr. Brown's famous school in present-day Barre. The members of the Barre Historical Society (which is pictured on the next page) were able to help me locate the remaining buildings, as well as guide me to information in their archive. I am extremely grateful for their assistance and hospitality when I visited Barre, Massachusetts.

This house was once Dr. Brown's family home (photograph by Dale Katovitch).

This building has undergone renovation since 1946. Members of the historical society described it as one of the early buildings of the school (photograph by Dale Katovitch).

Lucy Allen, a member of the Barre Historical Society, holding Catharine Brown's travel journal described in chapter 3. Lucy owns and is the transcriber of the journal.

Conclusion:
History Worth Mentioning

Stories work with people, for people, and always stories work on people, affecting what people are able to see as real, as possible, and as worth doing or best avoided. What is it about stories—what are their particularities—that enables them to work as they do? More than mere curiosity is at stake in this question, because human life depends on the stories we tell: the sense of self that those stories impart, the relationships constructed around shared stories, and the sense of purpose that stories propose and foreclose. (Frank 2010)

Discovering and writing the story of the Elm Hill School has been an adventure and a great privilege. It is a story that would have been lost if someone had simply discarded the records and photographs that are carefully preserved in Barre and Philadelphia. These documents are precious—there were many schools and institutions for people with intellectual and developmental disabilities, and any records that remain are aging and deteriorating. It would be a great shame to lose the stories of the students and staff.

However, most people with intellectual and developmental disabilities in the United States did not live in institutions. They remained in their communities. Where are those stories?

I have never asked anyone over the age of fifty if they have childhood memories of a family member, friend, or neighbor who had developmental disabilities and heard the answer, "No." Americans with intellectual disability were everywhere; their stories are not, and they are in danger of being lost forever. Elderly people who remember long-dead family members are dying themselves. Old photographs, letters, diaries, and scrapbooks are being thrown away. How can we save these treasures?

I've come to the conclusion that the majority of the stories will (and should) come from individuals with disabilities themselves, if possible, and if not, from their families, friends, and trusted caregivers. I consider it an ongoing part of my work to record and preserve these stories. Every story adds another layer of dimension and depth, even if the stories are incomplete. Some stories are tragic, and some are noble; most are simply ordinary. Some might think the stories too unimportant to relate, but think of the stories this way: as excited as archeologists are by a huge find, such as King Tut's tomb, they learn the most from the humble graves of ordinary Egyptian citizens. History is not just about the powerful.

The motto of the Museum of disABILITY History is a quote from historian William Lauren Katz: "If you believe that people have no history worth mentioning, it's easy to believe they have no humanity worth defending." We need to take this message seriously.

Technology has made preserving stories, documents, and pictures easy. There are smart phone apps that can record a conversation about the life of a relative or friend. Photographs can be scanned and stored for later generations.

I would also be delighted to help preserve your stories. If you are a person with intellectual and developmental disabilities or have memories of a family member, friend, neighbor, church member, etc., with such a disability, born in 1965 or before and would like to share their story, please contact me via email or social media at the addresses below.

Historyworthmentioning@gmail.com
Facebook.com/HistoryWorthMentioning

Resources

Annual Reports of the Elm Hill School: 1866, 1898 (25th Biennial Report), and 1900.

Bancroft, Hubert Howe (1893) *The Book of the Fair.* Chicago: The Bancroft Company.

Brown, Catharine (1887) "The Future of the Educated Imbecile." *The Proceedings of the Association of Medical Officers of American Institutions for Idiotic and Feeble-Minded Persons.* Philadelphia, PA: J.P. Lippincott Company.

Brown, Catharine (1897) "Reminiscences." *The Journal of Psycho-Asthenics.* Retrieved from http://www.disabilitymuseum.org/dhm/lib/detail.html?id=1578&page=all.

Brown, George (1887) "In Memoriam: Hervey B. Wilbur, M.D." *The Proceedings of the Association of Medical Officers of American Institutions for Idiotic and Feeble-Minded Persons.* Philadelphia, PA: J.P. Lippincott Company.

Brown, George (1887) "The Principles of Our Work." *The Proceedings of the Association of Medical Officers of American Institutions for Idiotic and Feeble-Minded Persons.* Philadelphia, PA: J.P. Lippincott Company.

Forbes, John (1847) *Medical Review or Quarterly Journal of Practical Medicine and Surgery,* 24.

Frank, Arthur (2010) *Letting Stories Breathe: A Socio-narratolgy.* Chicago: University of Chicago Press.

Institution for Idiots and Imbeciles, Barre, Massachusetts (1850) Friends' Review. Retrieved from disabilitymuseum.org/dhm/lib/detail.html?id=1364.

Kirisitis, Natalie, Platt, Douglas, and Stearns, Thomas (2013) *No Offense Intended: A Dictionary of Historical Disability Terms*. Buffalo, NY: People Ink Press.

Menace of the Feeble- Minded in Massachusetts, The (1913) Retrieved from www.archive.org/details/menaceoffeeblemiOOmass.

Osgood, Robert L. (2001) "The Menace of the Feebleminded: George Bliss, Amos, Butler, and the Indiana Committee on Mental Defectives." *Indiana Magazine of History, 97, 4 Proceedings of the Association of Medical Officers of American Institutions for Idiots and Feeble-Minded Persons* (1877). Philadelphia, PA: J.P. Lippincott Company.
Proceedings of the Association of Medical Officers of American Institutions for Idiots and Feeble-Minded Persons (1887) Philadelphia, PA: J.P. Lippincott Company

Rose, Sarah Frances (2008) *No Right to be Idle: The Invention of Disability 1850-1930* (Doctoral dissertation) Retrieved from ProQuest, Document number 30432950.

Seguin, Edward (1866) *Idiocy: And Its Treatment by the Physiological Method.* Albany, NY: Brandow Printing Company.

Stearns, Thomas E. (2014) *Path to the Institution: The New York State Asylum for Idiots*. Buffalo, NY: People Ink Press.

Trent, James W. Junior (1998) "Defectives at the World's Fair: Constructing Disability in 1904." *Remedial and Special Education* 19, 4.

Tyor, Peter L., and Bell, Leland V. (1984) *Caring for the Retarded in America: A History.* Westport, Connecticut: Greenwood Press.

Woodhouse, Rose (2012, April 8) The Moral Treatment, Hygiene, and Education of Idiots. Retrieved from ordinary-gentlemen.com/blog/2012/04/08/the-moral-treatment-hygiene-and-education-of-idiots/ent-hygiene-and-education-of-idiots/.

Acknowledgements

I would like to express my thanks to Syracuse University and the faculty and staff of the School of Education, for their ongoing support for this project.

This work would have been impossible without the archives of the Elm Hill School, carefully preserved and curated by the staff of the Historical Library of the College of Physicians of Philadelphia. The link to the finding aid is below. I made the most extensive use of boxes 10, 11, and 49–60, and the oversized student register.

Elm Hill Private School and Home for the Education of Feeble-Minded Youth records (Prepared by Charles Greifenstein, last updated November 10, 2011) Reference number MSS6/.0013-01

PACSCL Finding Aids - University of Pennsylvania

The records at the Barre Massachusetts Historical Society, and the kindness of the hardworking members, truly breathed life into the story of Dr. Brown's, and I am deeply grateful for their assistance and interest in helping to tell this story.

www.barremahistoricalsociety.org

In particular, I wish to thank, Margaret Marshall, Audrey Stevens, and Lucy Allen.

Books in Abandoned History Series:

On the Edge of Town: Almshouses of Western New York
by Lynn S. Beman and Elizabeth Marotta

Dr. Skinner's Remarkable School for "Colored Deaf, Dumb, and Blind Children" 1857 – 1860
by James M. Boles, EdD, and Michael Boston, PhD

When There Were Poorhouses: Early Care in Rural New York 1808 – 1950
by James M. Boles, EdD

An Introduction to the British Invalid Carriage 1850 – 1978 by Stuart Cyphus

Abandoned Asylums of New England
A Photographic Journey by John Gray
Historical Insight by the Museum of disABILITY History

No Offense Intended: A Directory of Historical Disability Terms
by Natalie Kirisits, Douglas Platt and Thomas Stearns

The Gold Cure Institutes of Niagara Falls, New York 1890s by James M. Boles, EdD

Of Grave Importance: The Restoration of Institutional Cemeteries
by David Mack-Hardiman

They Did No Harm: Alternative Medicine in Niagara Falls, NY 1830–1930
by James M. Boles, EdD

Path to the Institution: The New York State Asylum for Idiots
by Thomas E. Stearns

The Magic Fire: The Story of Camp Cornplanter
by David Mack-Hardiman

Buffalo State Hospital: A History of the Institution in Light and Shadow
A Photographic Journey by Ian Ference
Historical Insight by the Museum of disABILITY History

Books can be purchased in person at the Museum of disABILITY History Store, located inside the Museum at 3826 Main Street, Buffalo NY. Questions? Give us a call at 716.629.3626.

Can't make it in to the store? Check out the Museum Store online at store.museumofdisability.org.

Most books are available to purchase online as E-books through Amazon (Kindle) and Barnes and Noble (Nook).

CPSIA information can be obtained at www.ICGtesting.com
Printed in the USA
BVOW05s0818270816

460244BV00005B/5/P